Olly's Prison

An ordinary city flat. Evening. A man tries to talk to his daughter. She will not answer. And slowly their world turns to tragedy and a search begins that lasts for years. Many of the scenes are set in prison, but the greater prison lies outside. A vivid and powerful morality play for our time.

Olly's Prison was televised by the BBC in spring 1993. This volume includes the TV version and the stage adaptation.

D0988262

Edward Bond was born and educated in London. His plays include *The Pope's Wedding* (Royal Court Theatre, 1962), *Saved* (Royal Court, 1965), *Early Morning* (Royal Court, 1968), *Narrow Road to the Deep North* (Belgrade Theatre, Coventry, 1968; Royal Court, 1969), *Black Mass* (Sharpeville Commemoration Evening, Lyceum Theatre, 1970), *Passion* (CND Rally, Alexandra Palace, 1971), *Lear* (Royal Court, 1971), *The Sea* (Royal Court, 1973), *Bingo* (Northcott, Exeter, 1973; Royal Court, 1974), *The Fool* (Royal Court, 1975), *The Bundle* (RSC Warehouse, 1978), *The Woman* (National Theatre, 1978), *The Worlds* (New Half Moon Theatre, London, 1981), *Restoration* (Royal Court, 1981), *Summer* (National Theatre, 1982), *Derek* (RSC Youth Festival, The Other Place, Stratford-upon-Avon, 1982), *The Cat* (produced in Germany as *The English Cat* by the Stuttgart Opera, 1983), *Human Cannon* (Quantum Theatre, Manchester, 1986), *The War Plays* (*Red Black and Ignorant*, *The Tin Can People* and *Great Peace*) which were staged as a trilogy by the RSC at the Barbican Pit in 1985, *Jackets* (Leicester Haymarket, 1989), *September* (Canterbury Cathedral, 1989); *The Company of Men* (Paris, 1992); *Olly's Prison* (BBC 2 Television 1993); *Tuesday* (BBC Schools TV, 1993). His *Theatre Poems and Songs* were published in 1978 and *Poems 1978–1985* in 1987.

Edward Bond

Olly's Prison

METHUEN DRAMA

METHUEN MODERN PLAYS

First published in Great Britain 1993
by Methuen Drama
an imprint of Reed Consumer Books Ltd
Michelin House, 81 Fulham Road, London SW3 6RB
and Auckland, Melbourne, Singapore and Toronto

Copyright © 1993 by Edward Bond
The author has asserted his moral rights

ISBN 0–413–67610–2

A CIP catalogue record for this book
is available at the British Library

Typeset by Wilmaset Ltd, Birkenhead, Wirral
Printed in Great Britain by Cox & Wyman, Cardiff Road, Reading

Front cover photograph: Bernard Hill as Mike in the BBC TV production.
Photo by Willoughby Gullachsen, copyright © BBC Enterprises 1992.

Olly's Prison

Olly's Prison was first broadcast by BBC TV in spring 1993 with the following cast:

MIKE	Bernard Hill
SHEILA	Charlotte Coleman
VERA	Mary Jo Randle
FRANK	George Anton
BARRY	Bryan Pringle
SMILER	Jonny Lee Miller
PRISONER 1	Peter Sproule
PRISONER 2	Anthony Trent
PRISON OFFICER 1	Stuart Barren
PRISON OFFICER 2	Michael Irving
PRISON OFFICER 3	Charles Cork
ELLEN	Maggie Steed
OLIVER	Richard Graham

Also included in the cast were Dilly (a child), Dilly's mother and other prison visitors.

Directed by Roy Battersby
Produced by Richard Langridge

The play is set in London and the country, eleven years ago and in the present.

PART ONE

Section One – The Flat – Living-Room

A small living-room in a small block of working-class flats. There are three doors: one leads to the kitchen, another to the hallway between the living-room and the front door, and the third is a cupboard door. The cupboard and the door to the hallway are shut. A glass-fronted sideboard with a telephone on it. Fitted patterned carpet. Two armchairs and a bare table which is slightly larger than is usual in such a room. Its surface is slightly polished so that vague reflections appear in it. Four chairs are set at the table and in one of them SHEILA *sits with her forearms on the table. She is sixteen and is wearing a buttoned-up street coat. She does not move.*

Evening. Electric light.

Off, a sneeze from the kitchen.

MIKE *comes in from the kitchen in his stocking feet. He wears a pale shirt and grey trousers. He is in his late thirties.*

MIKE (*casually friendly*). Didnt hear you come in.

　　MIKE *goes out to the kitchen.*

MIKE (*off*). Good time?

　　SHEILA's *expression doesnt change.* MIKE *brings in an ornamental wastebin (bought at a stately home) and sets it down by the gas fire. He goes to the sideboard, opens a drawer, takes out a small ornamental place-mat, shuts the drawer and sets the place-mat on the table in front of* SHEILA.

MIKE. Going out again? Not this time a'night.

　　Off, a kettle starts to whistle. MIKE *goes out.* SHEILA *doesnt move.*

MIKE (*off*). Do the curtains.

　　Pause. MIKE *comes in with a cup of tea with a teabag and a teaspoon in it. He places it on the place-mat. He goes to the window and draws the curtains. His jacket is on the back of an armchair. He goes to it, takes a newspaper from a pocket, sits in the armchair and reads the newspaper.*

MIKE (*grumbling contentedly*). Not cold. Bloody ridiculous. (*He looks in the newspaper to see what's on.*) Heating's not going on this time a'year. Should eat properly. (*Still studying the newspaper.*) Lad left t'day. No job to go to. Didnt tell his missus. Be ructions round his place. (*Folds newspaper.*) You're no company. Quarrel with the boyfriend? Dont bring your troubles here and take it out on the home. (*He holds the folded newspaper as if he's going to let it fall open, but doesnt. Suddenly.*) Did you want to use the phone? Why didnt you say? I'll wait in the kitchen . . . (*No response.*) You're not talking to him either. (*Lets the newspaper fall open.*) Not leaving the room so you can sit and sulk. You've got your own room for that. Some people dont even have a roof. (*Shakes the newspaper as he prepares to read it.*) Sorry about the noise. (*Reads.*) Soon complain if I sat there. (*Looks up.*) Did I say something? (*No answer.*) I didnt start you off. Just being awkward. If I'd said something the whole world'd know by now. You're not working me up. Read the paper in peace. Im comfortable. (*Reads.*) That tea'll get cold. Lad just left . . . (*Still reading.*) If you could see yourself. That's a sign of real rotten ignorance. You're in a mood so you're entitled to impose it on everyone else.

MIKE *stops reading, lays the newspaper down open on his stomach like a sheet, lies back and shuts his eyes.*

MIKE. God I hate this carry-on. Work all day, come home, cook a meal, tidy up – then this. 'S not human. Dont you get enough of it outside? Least we can treat each other like human beings in our own place. Suppose I should've asked if you wanted it: 'Want a cup a' tea?' No one's forcing you to drink it. You heard the kettle. If you didnt want it you should've said. If something's bothering you tell me. I'll listen. If you're affected Im affected. Muggins pays in the end. You know what they're like round here. 'Why didnt you find out?' 'She wouldnt say.' 'Fine father!

– you're supposed to know not wait to be told.' D'you
want a doctor? (*Goes back to reading the newspaper.*) Be in
dead trouble then. He'd put you in a looney bin – that's
your trouble. Well this time you've chosen the wrong day.
You're not leaving this room till you drunk that tea.

Slight pause. MIKE *gets up, goes to the kitchen door and
closes it.*

MIKE. You're not the only one who can play at silly
buggers. Come too much of it!

MIKE *goes back to the armchair and sits.*

MIKE. I've got all night. You drink it before you leave this
room. (*Pause.*) I worked for this house. Not going to sit in
it and be treated like dirt. (*Pause.*) If you dont like it move
out. No one's stopping you. Do what you like in your own
place. Soon find out when the bills start coming in. Yeh,
that's what you'd like! Have a fine old time then! Well
you're not going. You can show a few signs of responsibi-
lity before I let you out of my jurisdiction. Not having
people say I let you live on the streets. That's where you'd
end up. While you're under my roof you live by the rules.
They're not hard. Just a bit of mutual consideration.

MIKE *gets up, goes to the table and feels the cup.*

MIKE. Be cold. Serve you right. (*Pause.*) You can have
some hot in if you like. Im not forcing you to drink cold
tea.

MIKE *goes to the middle of the room. He hesitates and looks
at* SHEILA.

MIKE. Let it stay there. You sit and think it over miss. I'll
phone the manageress in the morning and tell her you're
not coming in.

MIKE *goes to the armchair and sits.*

MIKE. Dont think I wouldnt! (*Pause.*) Talking t' meself.
(*Sudden rage.*) Drink the tea!

Slight pause. Suddenly MIKE *gets up, takes a chair from the table, goes to the kitchen door and wedges the back of the chair under the door handle. He goes to the armchair and sits.*

MIKE. Told you. Im not in the mood. (*Pause.*) And dont dribble it on the table to show us you're clever – dont mean a thing round here. If we cant treat each other with respect at least we can respect the furniture. That came out of this pocket. (*Slight pause.*) Not marking that. Turning the place into a pigsty. Suppose you want me to force you to drink it? Put me in the wrong. Slosh it down your coat so you can get a new one out of me. If I took it in my head I could get you out of that coat. I know fathers who'd pour it down your collar. Soon be out of it then! (*Pause.*) What d'you think my life's like? Too busy thinking about yourself. As long as I pay the bills, that's all you worry. I know I should've asked. I put myself in the wrong. That's no excuse for this carry on. Doesnt matter who started it. Im head of the household and Im asking you to stop it. (*Reads newspaper.*) Come in – not a dicky bird – I didnt bellyache – made a cup a' tea – a father making a nice friendly gesture, trying to behave in a civilized manner – I thought you'd like a cup a' tea and a chat, tell me what sort of day it was: you cant even say good evening! No this is a big joke! Laugh for your mates. Really chuffed if I chuck it in the sink and broke the cup. Well you're not getting me worked up. Entitled to peace in my own home. (*Pause.*) You're not a child now. Young lady your age in the house. We've got to adapt. (*Stops reading.*) How can I get it right if you dont give me a chance? Its not easy. (*Puts down the newspaper.*) We've got to sort ourselves out like a family. Well what's your suggestion? (*No response.*) Its the same with this tea. I let this drop, there'll only be a repetition t'morrow. It'll be back to square one. Stop it now before it gets out of hand.

Pause. MIKE *gets up and pushes the other armchair against the hallway door.*

MIKE. I know – bloody stupid: a cup a' tea! But Im going to have it drunk. Its only right.

MIKE *goes to the armchair and sits.*

MIKE. You wont go through that door till. (*Pause.*) I'd fall asleep on me way to bed. What do I get out of sitting here? Nothing on, missed the forecast. I've got to go in t'morrow even if it is Saturday. Drink it up like a good girl.

MIKE *gets up, goes to the table and sits in a chair facing* SHEILA.

MIKE. You know I worry. If your mother was alive she'd talk to you. Table too big. Bargain. Couldnt afford to let it go. Sat here when she was ill. Didnt go in the armchair case I didnt wake up when she called. What's the use of talking *back*? – 'nough trouble *now*. I talk to make you talk. It just shuts you up. Wont get a word now I mentioned your mother. That put the lock on the lid. God you cried when she died. The water didnt pour out your eyes like a kid. Poured out your whole face. I thought it was broken – skin ruptured or something – and the water poured out the cracks. When you lose something like that you lose touch with everything. Think it's all going. I wiped the tears off and your face was still there. You looked different – as if you'd been crying for all your mates. I felt ashamed of bringing you into the world. Let me put your coat on a hanger. Nice on you. Shame to let it crease. Hope the boyfriend appreciates it. Suppose you dont want me to touch you . . .

MIKE *goes back to his armchair and sits.*

MIKE. Pour it down the sink. Drink it under threat you'll be ill – end up with tummy ulcers. Pour it down the sink, wash the cup and hang it on the dresser. That wont make you ill. So now there's no excuse. It comes down to your attitude.

MIKE *goes to the kitchen door and takes the chair away from it. He goes to his armchair and sits.*

MIKE. Now we'll see.

Pause. Suddenly MIKE *twists so that he's lying on his side facing away from* SHEILA, *with his legs stretched straight out and the upper part of his body hunched forward. His eyes are shut.*

MIKE. . . . If you were a knife you wouldnt need lessons in sharpness. Perhaps you should go and live with the boyfriend. See if he can knock some sense into you. I dont blame *you*. What can you know at your age? The welfare said have you adopted. No, you think, love comes first. Times I wished she'd died before we had you. Least we'd be spared this. You work hard, try, where does it get you? You dont even know what's in their heads. I dont even know if you're listening. Are you still there? Perhaps you had the sense to walk out? – its finished. Im too bloody tired to open my eyes. Day after day the same. Why did I bring your mother into it? Bloody whiner . . .

MIKE *opens his eyes and turns to look:* SHEILA *sits as before.*

MIKE. I wish you'd gone Sheila. Its such a pity.

MIKE *gets up, pushes the armchair against the halldoor so that its blocked. Then he wedges the back of the chair under the handle of the kitchen door and sits in it.*

MIKE. Stupid. Stupid. This bloody chair. (*He runs his hands through his hair.*) You're really going for it tonight. You're out of your depth. Im not giving in. Arent you ashamed of doing this to your father? – look at me. (*Suddenly sardonic.*) Did I serve it in the wrong cup? I feel sorry for you. Off you go in your new coat – nose in the air – clippity-clip – not a thought in your head. If you could see yourself, you're like a dog dragging its kennel round on a chain. Right: you've got half a minute. (*His watch.*) Twenty seconds. (*Pause.*) Eleven. Ten. Nine.

After another twenty seconds he goes to the table. With the teaspoon he presses the teabag against the side of the cup, lifts it out, carries it across the room and throws it into the wastebin.

MIKE. In.

MIKE *goes back to the table and puts the teaspoon next to the teacup on the place-mat.*

MIKE. You will drink it. There's got to be some order. (*He leaves the table.*) We're barricaded in.

Pause. MIKE *goes back to the table and picks up the teacup.*

MIKE. God! – there's a ton of it. Heavy! That's what arguing does. You wouldnt have the strength to lift it! Right: Im holding it up for you. (*He puts the teacup to her mouth.*) That's the most I'll do. Its up to you. You dont have to drink it all. Let me see you take one sip. Then we'll forget it. One sip. Try. Shall I take a sip? Its not poisoned. No that's not why you wont. You could've said at the start 'Dad I dont want a drink' – 'Sure luv that's okay' – I'd've drunk the lot. Now its too late. Gone beyond that. Its not a cup a' tea any more. (*He puts down the teacup.*) No you wont will you? You have to go on with it.

MIKE *goes back to the armchair and sits.*

MIKE. My hand didnt shake when I lifted the cup. (*Pause.*) You think t'morrow there'll be some smart alec way out. You'll want a sub so you'll *have* to talk. 'Scared me with the chairs dad. Upset me over mum.' That worked in the past Sheila, it won't work t'morrow. Be careful. You could be sitting in a room with a lunatic. Its all got on top of me. Run up debts. Got the sack. Off me head. You dont know. All sorts of things happen these days. (*Pause.*) Must be some sort of satisfaction being as ignorant as you. If you were a pig you wouldnt know the smell of muck. You think its big to say no. Anyone can do that. I pity your kids. What sort of future d'you think you're making for them? Perhaps people cant learn any more – put on the headphones and shut it out. People dying – being robbed – going crazy – and you sit. The world's being handed over to people like you – and you dont even know your own street. You're nothing really, because you dont *want* to understand. If you did you'd be on your knees begging me to help you – talk to you. You changed our whole lives this evening Sheila. You'll drink the tea but it wont repair the damage. If you only knew, you're running round this room putting a wall across it – you cant chuck the bricks up fast enough. I can see you from the cradle to the grave. When you marry – have kids – get old – you'll still be in that chair. You'll end up like the little old woman down the road. She lives in a corner of her room behind a wall of bags. When they want her they call her out as if she's an animal in a hole. Why why why did I mention your mother? That's the one thing I blame myself for . . . You're more dead than she is. Your sort of stubbornness is worse than being dead. You want to run the world? – one cup of tea – under your nose – and you cant put out your hand. You're trapped. Well well well.

MIKE *twists to one side, as before, and shuts his eyes but his shoulders do not hunch.*

MIKE. I've seen real pain. Grown-up people crying. You cant help, cant do anything. An old man in the papers. They found him sitting straight up on a box. The skin crumbling off like paint – falling off like feathers on a bird flat in the road. His tongue was hanging out like a toilet roll. He'd forgotten his own language . . . Why'm I telling you this? Take your arms off the table. This wont blow over t'morrow. It'll take more than that. All this for one cup of tea. Its terrible.

MIKE *jumps up and goes to the table.*

MIKE. Arms off! You want me to knock them off! – fight! Then you've got bruises to show. Go round in short sleeves – put powder on 'em to pretend you dont want 'em to show and make sure the whole street stinks of powder for weeks!

MIKE *pulls the table away from* SHEILA. *Her hands fall into her lap.*

Ha! Ha! Gotcher! Didnt think of that! The table moved! The world doesnt always do what you want it to! Bang! Now she knows what the mouse feels when it goes for the cheese! I'd've liked the privilege of being inside her head when the table moved! And I didnt spill a drop! (*He sits in the armchair blocking the hallway door.*) Have to be childish when you're dealing with a child. Bang! (*He calms down.*) . . . The lad just left. The shift didnt make a collection. Not even voluntary redundancy – self-inflicted. Why should they put their hands in their pockets? Could go off an do the same the next place. Make a regular racket . . . I nearly went to Australia. Then I met your mother. Everything changed. Work offered me training plus a rise at the end. Then its all over. I never hit you. I pinched the top of your arm when I was putting you in your school coat and you dawdled. I darent be late. You could've drunk the tea. It wasnt much to ask. No you wont. Too easy. Got to be the hard way. A tragedy. One cup of tea and the world's got to end.

MIKE *goes to* SHEILA *and stands behind her chair. He picks it up with her in it and places it at the table where it was before. Her hands are in her lap. The tea is in front of her.*

MIKE. Where there's a will. Pushed your pram for hours. Row of little dollies on the hood. Made out of wool on a string. Had the hood up even when it was sunny. Washed you. Ugly little toes. Put you to bed. Dished your food up on the plate – I made the tea out of habit. Said 'eat it up, its good' and you believed it. Had more sense then. Now I say be a good girl – drink it up – its good because it'll get us out of the mess – you wont. Its all got to go in the bin. If you drink it *I'd* taste it. You watch a mother feed a kid. She scoops the grub up on the spoon – shoves it in its little gob – and goes gobble-gobble as if *she's* enjoying it. Even has to wipe her chin. Daft. If she didnt do it we'd still be in caves . . . 'Drink your tea or it'll swallow you up!'. Once you said 'If I eat it will mummy come back?' If it was that simple. . . . I didnt mean it about a wall. People hurt each other all the time – you'd think that's what we're here for – but you live through it. We dont have to punish each other for surviving.

MIKE *pulls the chair and armchair from the doors and leaves them haphazardly in the centre of the room. He picks up the teacup and goes out to the kitchen.* SHEILA *doesnt move. After a moment* MIKE *comes back with the teacup. He puts it where it was on the table.*

MIKE. Made some tea. Nice evening?

MIKE *sits in his armchair.*

MIKE. No its not that easy. Only the other way now. With pain. You're right: I put you on the spot, I've got to stick with it. Its worse than that. All this damage . . . when you drink it you'll make it worse. You'll drink it like an insult. Like spitting it in my face. A cup of tea. That decides now. Have you heard a word I said? Dont even know if you saw the table move. I wish it wasnt late. Before you get into this you need time to finish. No use after midnight. Talk. Nothing's done. Threats. Crawling for sympathy. If I hadnt – !: why why why did I bring your mother into it? That's the last tea I make you. The lad just left.

Help me Sheila. You dont know what's happening. People are cruel. I dont know why. They make you suffer. What we're in now – this teacup – that'll happen all your life. One way or another. That's all there is. Learn to handle it. You've got a chance. In a few years its over. I try to help you – talk and talk – we're the only people in the room – and I cant tell you – because you wont have it! Something's got to be done. (*He goes to the table.*) Sheila I made the tea and put it on the table. That's an order. (*Wanders off.*) No she wont. I said one sip. I held the cup. She wont, she wont.

MIKE *goes to the table and sits.*

MIKE. Drink it. Please. *Please.* Will that do? (*Sprawls with his head on the table, bangs the table with his fists.*) Help me. A daughter should. We lived here sixteen years – we wont fight over a cup! For nothing! Give me your hand. *Dont* understand! If its hard! No need for a reason! Give me your hand (*Pushes her hand towards the cup. She doesnt respond.*) Touch it. Touch it. Something must belong in this world. Something must have its place! (*He stares at the cup, holds one hand round it as if he's protecting a candle-flame and hammers his other fist next to it on the table.*) Take it! Take it! Something take it! Smash it! Smash it! No no there's nothing! No help! (*The side of his head is on the table. He draws his neck into his shoulders.*) The wood on my face. I cant see. I wont look. Cant. You wont lose. Drink it. *Dont* drink it! Say! Just say! Lie! Lie! Lie! Say you drank it! (*He gets up and leaves the table. Turns to face her.*) Tell me you drank it! (*No response. Violently.*) Drink! Drink! Drink! Help me! Help me! No no . . . (*Rapid mutter.*) No she wont the hard-faced little bitch – grinning inside her head – she'd let it stand there on her mother's grave till its colder than the corpse. A laugh. The bitch. The dirty little bitch. (*Looks at* SHEILA. *Pleads.*) Sheila . . . is it too much to ask? Then what! Pick up a spoon? Shut the door? Too much! (*Mutter.*) You brought her in the world. What'll you do about it? I'll do what I must do! You cant! I will! (*Pleads.*) Sheila! . . . My god one day you'll ask and no one'll listen! You're my child – you hard-faced little slut . . . You bitch! I will! I will! They kick you out of doors and make you shut it! (*He goes behind the chair.*) My child, my child!

MIKE *slams his hands round* SHEILA's *neck, lifts her straight up out of the chair and strangles her. For a moment she is too shocked to react. Then her hands go up and claw at his hands. Her body wrenches round once so that it is sideways to the table – the chair comes round with her. The shape of her body is contained in his body as if they were one piece of sculpture. The struggle is concentrated and intense – their bodies shake, vibrate, violently judder – like a magnified drop of water on the end of an icicle before it falls. Her hands claw more weakly, they seem to be patting his hands. No sound except breathing. The camera has moved in slowly but stopped while they are both full-length.*

When SHEILA *is dead* MIKE *lowers her into the chair. She*

*sits bolt upright, sideways to the table. He moves away. After
a moment he looks at the table. He goes towards it. Stops.
Turns to the kitchen. Stops. Goes to SHEILA. He picks up
the chair – with her in it – and turns it to face the table. The tea
is in front of her as before. He goes to the armchair and sits on
the arm.*

MIKE. Drink your tea. (*He glances vaguely at his arms as if
they hurt.*) Phew! . . . That chair's . . . well . . . I told you
what would –. Work in the morning. The lad just left.
Come on Sheila. (*He gets up and goes to the table.*) Sugar.
Diet. Boyfriend. Its in now, drink up. You might as well.

MIKE *sits at the table and puts his hands in his lap.*

MIKE (*Gently*). I dont want us to come to any – Im sorry if
I –. I'll put the kettle on and –. Dont punish me. You
were so quiet. Perhaps you're still . . . ? I cant put out my
hand to see. Afraid, in case –.

MIKE *stands, picks up the cup and goes towards the kitchen.
Stops.*

MIKE. She doesnt have to be –. No need. That can be said
when its time. (*Cradles the cup.*) You can pretend it hasnt
happened. (*Calm amazement. Flat.*) How wonderful. The
room – the night – all this – its free. How wonderful to live
here. (*Tears.*) So lucky . . . (*Hurries to the table.*) There
was – there – was –. (*He finds the teaspoon, fills it with tea
and holds it to* SHEILA'*s mouth.*) If you could drink. To
help . . . No she wont. Stubborn. (*Tea dribbles.*) O Sheila
your new coat. The money. Ruined. What will she be
buried in! Bills. Bills.

MIKE *goes to the sideboard, opens a drawer, takes out
envelopes, stamps, a chequebook, a biro and a few bills. He
goes to the table and sits.*

MIKE. Sort all this. Bills. Bills. Electricity. Estimate again.
(*Writes cheque.*) I should complain. Call when we're in.
Bills. What's this. Your credit card. More shoes. (*He is
going to write another cheque. Stops.*) She's dead. You must

let it happen. Her right. Be fair. Its all she's got. (*To* SHEILA.) I took the rest. All that – So easy. (*Touches her arm.*) Can you feel my – ? Perhaps it takes a little time to go. They'll punish me. Is that what you want to hear? The last words. They're true. I wouldnt lie to you now. Our life isnt that bad. The last words must be true. Perhaps you're screaming at me: 'Bastard! Bastard! Killer!' Dont! I called you slut. I thought I had more time to –. Bills. Bills. These are facts. Milk? (*He tries to read a bill but puts it down.*) It doesnt matter.

He puts the cheque in an envelope and seals it. He gets up and goes to the window, lifts the curtain and peers out.

MIKE. Empty. All asleep. Wake up in the morning. Then the fuss. Your coat's caught on the chair. You used to watch here for me when I came home.

MIKE *switches off the light. Street lighting comes through the curtains. He sits in the armchair and immediately goes to sleep.* SHEILA *sits bolt upright in front of the tea.*

Section Two – Living-Room and Hallway

Morning. Daylight comes through the drawn curtains. SHEILA lies face down on the table with the cup beside her. MIKE sleeps slumped in the armchair. A doorbell. He does not react. A few moments pass and he opens his eyes and concentrates, trying to recall if he has heard a sound. The doorbell again. He gets up, notices the curtains are drawn and opens them. He goes out into the hallway.

MIKE *walking to the front door. He opens it. Beyond him* VERA, *a neighbour. She is about thirty and is in indoor clothes.*

VERA. Rang four times. Standing there. Your curtains are drawn.
MIKE. What time is it?
VERA (*coming along the corridor towards the camera*). You'll be asking me what day it is next. Thought you were

working this weekend. I cant stop. Came to see Sheila. She up?

MIKE's *face: he remembers. He starts after* VERA.

MIKE. No no she's not – you cant –

VERA *is entering the living-room followed by* MIKE. SHEILA *is slumped as before.*

VERA. She drunk? She's not starting all that? Sheila . . . !
MIKE. Leave her.
VERA (*picks up the teacup*). Eugh! She come home in that state? No wonder you didnt want to let me in.

VERA *speaks in a low voice.* MIKE *copies her.*

MIKE. Im going out.
VERA. And you – all crumpled! Suppose *you* slept like that. Fine pair!
MIKE. Got to go out.
VERA. I was on my balcony and saw your curtains. The frowse in this room! (*She goes to the window.*)
MIKE. Dont.
VERA (*opens the window*). Let some honest-to-goodness pollution in.
MIKE. I've got to go to work –
VERA. Im glad I caught her like that. (*She glances at the bills.*) Poor kid. She needs another woman – with a bit of experience. Talk about make-up – clothes – have a good row. A man's no use. Dont worry, she cant hear. If they dont have someone they turn in on themselves. Dont say you havent been warned.
MIKE. What did you want? Is there anything – ?
VERA. You're half her trouble. More than half. (*Shrug.*) Its none of my business. You let me know where the line is. That was made very clear from the start. Im useful for the washing and tidying – and your visit once a week – and even then you dont always stay after. You wouldnt find many women so understanding. (*Shrug.*) I accepted it. Im not being used. Its more than that.
MIKE. I cant listen. Im late.

VERA. She hasnt got a mother – and she's only got half a father. You're all over the place – so what's she got to cling to?

MIKE (*trying to explain*). Vera something I – I want –

VERA. I should be here full time. That's what both of you need. You wouldnt have to cope with it all on your own. We ought to get married. Why *dont* we?

MIKE. I cant talk about that – I've got to –

VERA. This isnt a good life. Tell me what rights we've got? We cant make demands on each other. Im allowed to worry and fret and that's all. Im not even entitled to that. Half the time Im afraid to open my mouth. If I cried I'd be told to mind my own business. Its no different for you. We let everything go to waste. Well you're certainly in no hurry to answer.

MIKE. I cant think now.

VERA. Dont give me that. (*Sour.*) This has gone through your head more than once. You've got your answer ready! (*Tries to reconcile.*) There isnt anyone else. And Im not trying to replace your wife – that only happens once. But she's dead. We're not teenagers, we dont expect the earth. There'd be two salaries coming in. Why dont I shut up? Her lying there seemed the golden opportunity. She makes my point for me. I should keep it to myself! We'll go on as before. I think you deserve better.

MIKE. Keep it to yourself? You're always saying it!

VERA (*idea*). Unless you're planning to ask her permission? Even you wouldnt be so daft! Girls that age are little madams when it comes to being jealous. An older woman in the house – she wouldnt get her own way all the time. O I wont shut her out – I know my responsibilities. But I wouldnt encourage *this* for a – (*Stops suddenly.*) When did I say it before?

MIKE. What?

VERA. You said Im always saying –

MIKE. Last week – a few weeks back – ! You're always hinting – going on –

VERA. No Im not! Its been on my mind – I dont deny it –

but that's why I know what I said. I went out of my way
not to say! – so I couldnt be accused. Now this! You're
twisting my words. I said she'd move out when –

MIKE. It doesnt matter!

VERA. It matters to me! A lot! Always saying? Hinting?
You make me sound like a –. I dont have to go begging for
it!

MIKE. Its always something! Who shut the window? That
wasnt you? O god I'll go mad. Leave me alone. I've got to
go.

VERA. The woman on my landing's selling her carpets. (*She
gives the teacup to* MIKE.) Sheila was thinking of one to go
by the bed. (*She picks up the sealed envelope.*) D'you want
anything if I pass by the shops?

MIKE. No no.

VERA (*takes the teacup from him*). And Im right. You'll see.
When she's ready she'll be off.

VERA *goes into the kitchen.* MIKE *puts the envelopes,
stamps, chequebook, biro and bills into the drawer. He closes
it.* VERA *comes back without the teacup.*

VERA. I've come up here cleaning six years. I know your
dust better than I know my own. You've never given me a
key. All that time. (*Envelope.*) I'll post this. Im only
thinking of your convenience. One of you wouldnt always
have to be in for me. Shall I have a key cut?

MIKE *shuts the window.*

VERA. Dont know how you can live in it. And dont shout at
me again! 'S not human after I've shown my feelings! Will
you come down in the week?

MIKE. I've got to go.

VERA. Well its not my place. I've no rights here.

MIKE. Thanks about the carpets.

VERA. I might not be in.

VERA *goes out into the hallway. The front door is heard
closing.* MIKE *hesitates a moment. He goes behind* SHEILA
to the cupboard. He opens the cupboard door.

It is full of neatly stacked domestic appliances and stores – a radio, vacuum cleaner, hair dryer, portable electric fire, a box of Christmas decorations, bottles of cleaners, dusters, etc. Clothes on hangers on the walls. In a corner at the back a set of mail-order luggage. MIKE pulls out the biggest case.

MIKE leaves the cupboard door open. He puts the suitcase down by SHEILA. He opens it but immediately turns away and goes to the phone. He dials. Waits.

MIKE. Frank please. (*Pause.*) Did you row? Mike. When Sheila came in, she –. Come here. You must! Now! (*Pause.*) All right, Im sorry. Its not important. Yes yes. This evening. Thank you. Yes.

Section Three – Living-Room
'The Hand on the Telephone'

That evening. Darkish. MIKE is getting up from the armchair. He goes out to the hallway. Off, the sound of the front door.

FRANK (*off*). Well what was so urgent?

MIKE follows FRANK into the room. FRANK is in his early twenties. He wears dark trousers, a green shirt and a maroon blouson.

FRANK. Sheila? (*To MIKE.*) Is she all right?

FRANK puts on the electric light.

MIKE. She's dead.
FRANK (*trying to understand*). Ill is – ? The doctor? Mike? (*He goes towards SHEILA.*)
MIKE (*stopping him with his voice*). I killed her.
FRANK. O yeh you and Jack the Ripper? You're paying me back. Both of you. (*He tiptoes towards SHEILA, miming holding a dagger.*) I've got a nasty big knife to –
MIKE. Aah!
FRANK (*realises*). O no. (*Goes to phone.*)
MIKE. Dont! An arrangement's got to be made.

FRANK. You said you'd –

MIKE. A cup of tea.

FRANK (*goes towards* MIKE). You – have you sat there all day with – ? (*Squeezes* MIKE's *arm*.) You didnt kill her. O you poor –. You disturbed someone and – the shock. (*Sees the suitcase.*) Look they were –. A cup of tea?

MIKE. I forgot.

FRANK (*realises*). No you wouldnt sit there all day if you'd disturbed a. . . . (*Goes to phone.*) Tell me. Its quiet. When I phone they'll all come. What did you put in her tea?

MIKE. Terrible things have happened here. Terrible. I didnt know they – you could be pushed so far.

FRANK. The tea!

MIKE. Last night. Was it? We rowed. I slept. The door. And I forgot!

FRANK (*watch*). You've got half a minute.

MIKE. I killed her and forgot! Forgot! Forgot!

FRANK. It was someone else. (*Dialling.*) The police'll know what to –

MIKE. The arrangement! Take the flat. (FRANK *stops dialling.*) I sat here all day. I worked it out. You can afford the gas and electricity and upkeep and the tax. There's no mortgage. It was a struggle. The interest was higher than they said. I dont know what happens to your stuff when you've done this. Get a lawyer. Make it legal. Its worth the cost. Say we arranged it weeks ago in case it makes a difference. Im sorry I shouted. I was afraid you might not want it because she died here. You cant afford to think like that. I've lost everything. (God Im an evil bastard!) Take the flat. Then something's saved. Yes you will – I can see from your hand on the phone.

FRANK. You mean the freehold? Not a lease?

MIKE. Yes.

FRANK. I always liked this flat. (*Doubt.*) Wait. What if people say Im mixed up in the . . . ? Its your idea. You said to help you.

MIKE. It would've been hers one day. So when you married . . .

FRANK. She'd've wanted me to have it. I cant believe she's dead . . . People my age dont often get a chance to own their place. I need some cover. If you change your mind – I warn you –

MIKE. I forgot.

FRANK. Scribble something down for the lawyer.

MIKE. I'll do it.

FRANK. Its furnished too.

MIKE (*dismisses him*). . . . Now call the police . . .

PART TWO

Section One – Visiting Room in a Closed Prison

*Day. The room is partitioned with a barrier across which visitors
and prisoners talk. Two wardens – one on a high stool – watch by
the door.*

VERA *and* MIKE *face each other.*

VERA. I didnt bring anything. Didnt know you could.
   Should've come before. Dont know where all the time
   went. I had to sort it out in my head. Decide what to do
   with my own life. I'll stand by you. The man said I
   could've brought magazines in.

MIKE. Long journey.

VERA. Nothing's changed. The flats are still there. You
   know Frank's got a new girl?

MIKE. He didnt keep in touch.

VERA. I'll never know how you . . . You're not a violent
   person. We all lose our temper. How could you kill your
   daughter? . . . It was the stairs. Me downstairs, you up.
   You had a row. If I'd been there to say wait a minute . . .
   she'd be alive. If I'd just come up to borrow something!

MIKE. Frank's got a new girl?

VERA. I want us to get married.

MIKE. Vera Im here for life.

VERA. That's only their way of putting it.

MIKE. Its nine or ten years minimum. Or twice as long.
   They can change the rules when they like.

VERA. You're not putting me off this time.

MIKE. No no. This is my life. No past, nothing in front of
   yer, just day t' day. Its the only way t' survive. If I've got
   another life out there I could still be living *if* I 'adnt . . .
   The world ends at that door.

VERA. The time'll go –

MIKE. Stop it!

VERA. – then what? You'll be a lost kid – come out and grab
   the first hand you see. Gods knows what sort of woman'll

get her claws into you. You cant look after yourself – it was all pretence. That's why you're here.

MIKE. That's 'outsider' talk! If I thought like that I'd go round the bend.

VERA. I'll be waiting with a home. You wont have to worry your secret'll be found out. Im doing it for me as well as you. Im not an angel.

MIKE. Why did you ave t' come ere? I stopped meself thinkin. Chriss woman cant yer see what yer've done? I could be in that room with 'er body now! Why did yer come?

VERA. More self pity. You'd feel sorry for yourself if you won the pools. Im glad I never met your wife.

MIKE. Dont talk about her!

VERA. You put her on a pedestal. If you worship someone dead the rest of us are bound to seem shop-soiled: we've got to cope with life. Your wife put you here.

MIKE. O go away.

VERA. She's in the cemetery and you're in prison – isnt that far enough apart? I've learned a lot these last few months. If you cant be free in here you never will be. (*Gently.*) You're a good man. None of this should've happened. You do what you say: go on day t' day and forget everything. It'll be like falling asleep for a long rest. Its a fairy story. You'll be away so long all the nasty things'll vanish. The past never happened. When you wake up you'll be cured. Forget *me*. I'll be so busy it'll be enough for both of us. I'll live your life for you. Im glad you're in prison. I can see the way clear now. I blame her for Sheila's death – but I thank her for bringing us together. When I saw the warders in their uniform at the gate I wanted to rush up and kiss them. I felt so safe.

MIKE. I forgot.

VERA. What did you forget luvvy?

MIKE. I was with her body all night. Then you rang and I opened the door. I forgot she was there. I didnt know I was a murderer.

VERA. Of course not. If you were wicked you'd've known.

That sort of person has their wits about them. Last thing they do is let anyone in.

MIKE. I forgot.

VERA. Shock.

MIKE. I could've gone out to work – or Timbuctoo. I wouldnt'a known till someone told me. If I'd killed a stranger – there'd be no one t' tell me.

VERA. What magazines d'you want?

MIKE. If you can forget for one night – with the body under your feet – you can forget for the rest of your life. Its terrible. It just drops out of your mind –

VERA. Dont talk daft.

MIKE. – an' yer think you're innocent! There's people walkin round who've done terrible things an' dont –

VERA. Stop it.

MIKE. *You* might think you're innocent only because yer dont know what you've done!

VERA. I beg your pardon? I didnt come here for all this tommy rot! You murdered your daughter! She's in her grave. You had a proper trial. You're in prison. I dont want to hear another word.

MIKE. How could I forget?

VERA. I told you: shock. You frighten me when you're like this. Its not right. Havent we suffered enough to satisfy you? I've got to go back on the train with all this whizzing round in my head. You sit here ten years thinking up any more of this and they'll never let you out! You murdered your daughter.

MIKE. I know.

VERA. Then dont accuse me. Telling me I dont know what I've done! There's nothing to be ashamed of in my life – unless its slaving for you! Im not sitting here being accused. When I rang your bell I didnt know you had a body inside. You could've let me in and strangled *me*! Then I suppose you'd've forgot! I never blamed you. Came here and offered to devote myself – like a bloody fool! *You murdered your daughter*. Say it to yourself every day. Its your only chance. If we cant face what we've done we'll all end up murderers! You always make me sound so harsh. Its a real gift. You dont know the hurt you cause.

MIKE (*flatly*). I didnt say I didnt do it. I did. Then I forgot. That's worse.

VERA. If you'd been murdered you wouldnt need the police to tell you. I suppose this is why you gave Frank the flat. Yes, let's have it all out! You gave Frank the flat because you forgot me? That it? How could you give it to him?

MIKE. Didnt think I –

VERA. I dont want to know! It'll only be more rubbish. Not that Im entitled to ask. Blast, blast! I promised myself I wouldnt mention it. Getting involved in all this worry for nothing! – Why did you give Frank the flat?

MIKE. To get shot of it.

VERA. The other flats said you did it to stop him killing you when he found Sheila's body. Anyway his new girl's moved in. You've got a stranger there now.

MIKE (*shrug.*) Its his place.

VERA. I *know*. (*Slight pause.*) Some of them said its not right him having another woman there. I hope its not haunted. (*Half-shrug.*) Well you cant live on spilt milk. The first visit was bound to be difficult. You're like a minefield. If someone looks at you you blow up in their face.

MIKE. . . . I could've walked out in the street – got lost in all that out there – gone to bed. It was easy. Why? Why? (*Cries.*)

VERA (*silently watches him cry. Pause*). I've nothing against Frank or his girl. I told her to change the wallpaper. She always let me in when I knocked, till Frank stopped it. I remind him of Sheila. You men only know how to love ladies when we're dead, dont you. Then you soon know how to cry for yourself. They wont stay in the flat. Some stains you cant wash out. We'll wait till it gets to him.

MIKE. Sorry. I'll be all right next time. You will come Vera? Please. And write. (*Tearfully puts his hand on hers.*) You've been a saint to me. I dont deserve it.

VERA. As long as you behave. No more pretending. I cant go on like that. Cry. You have to cry to get used to these

places. I can manage the fare once a month. I worked it
out. There are other things to save for.

Section Two – Association Area

*Day. A bleak space with doors and a cupboard. Tables, chairs
and a few games.*

*It is empty except for MIKE and BARRY sitting at adjoining
tables. MIKE is turned away with a vacant expression.
SMILER comes in. He seems under twenty and is blond, good-
looking and at home in the world. He crosses the Association
Area with a mug of tea.*

SMILER. Late for din-dins. (*Warning.*) Closin the 'atch.
BARRY. Smiler?
SMILER. Drop dead.
BARRY. *One*. Go on!

SMILER goes out through the far door.

BARRY (*mutter*). Little runt. (*Looks at MIKE.*) You're
bloody depressin. That cow stopped visitin yer? Yer give
'er the push. Should'a let 'er come. Somethin t' look at, bit
a' sniff. Dont 'ave t' listen. (*No answer.*) Your fourth year.
Always the worst. Cant 'elp, cant say nothin. Used t' think
the clock 'ad died.

*SMILER comes back without the mug and crosses the
Association Area towards the other door.*

BARRY (*offers*). Give yer three? Cant offer fairer. Be a sport.
SMILER (*crossing.*) You owe me two weeks.
BARRY. I'll settle up.

*SMILER stops and leans on the back of a chair at another
table: arms straight, left knee bent, left toe behind right heel.*

SMILER. Dont try your duff tricks on me grandad. Fly
little bleeder. Im the lad 'oo sells the worms t' the early
dickybirds. Out next week, so yer reckon yer wont 'ave t'

pay me. News for you. Wait till yer see 'oo's running the bag when Im gone.

BARRY. 'Oo?

SMILER. Ain nice natured like me when it comes t' owin – or anythin else.

BARRY. Give us a ciggie Smiler. Im bloody dyin.

SMILER. Congratulations – only go an do it outside in the dustbin. When yer goin t' settle?

BARRY. Its all arranged.

SMILER. You couldnt arrange a knife an fork if the plate gave yer lessons.

BARRY. Givvus.

SMILER. Scrougin git. You wouldnt show your arse to a blindman if it'd restore 'is sight – which ain likely.

BARRY. Farewell pressie?

SMILER. Pressie? If I was Santa Claus an you was the last Christmas tree on earth I wouldnt give yer a shovel of reindeer manooer. You owe me fifty-five.

BARRY. So what difference's one more?

SMILER. Geriatric old scrounger.

BARRY. Givvus a ciggie. (*Points to* SMILER's *shirt pocket*.) 'Ole bloody packet there! Look at it! Could put out me 'and an' touch it. (*Dry tears*.) I'll pay. I promise.

SMILER. Look at 'im pretendin t' cry. Got runny eyes lookin through key'oles.

BARRY (*rage*). 'F I wanna be a fool, thass *my* right! I take what's comin when I cant pay. Never 'ear me whine! (*Softening. Wheedles*.) You're a vicious little turd Smiler. I bet all the best sewers put in bids for you. Be a pal, givvus. I settled it with Clarkie. 'E pays what 'e owes on the trannie an I pay you. 'E give 'is word.

SMILER. Never 'eard you whine? You sound like a fart that cant afford music lessons. Shouldnt put young blokes with you geriatric trash. Corruptin the nation's future.

MIKE *gets up and slowly walks out*.

BARRY. Just one. Keep me goin. Avent 'ad a ciggie since slop out.

SMILER *takes the cigarette packet from his shirt pocket.*

BARRY. Good lad! Knew yer wouldnt let a mate go without.

SMILER *takes a cigarette from the packet. Then he fishes down behind the cigarettes and takes out a thin blade.*

BARRY. You sod! Yer dirty little toe-rag! Yer'd steal the maggots off a corpse.

SMILER *lays the cigarette packet, the cigarette and the blade in a neat row on the edge of the table. Surveys them.*

SMILER (*offer*). Yes or no?

BARRY. Yeh yeh. Givvus. You'll want one day. I wouldnt lend you a straight corkscrew.

SMILER. If it was straight yer wouldnt know what it was. You're so bent yer bump in t' yerself comin back.

SMILER *cuts the cigarette in two with the blade.*

SMILER. Like a tit in a baby's gob.

BARRY (*walking up and down in agitation*). When you was born yer mother only let yer live cause she'd run out a' toilet roll.

SMILER *holds up the two halves to measure them against each other. With quiet satisfaction he finds they are exactly the same length.*

SMILER. Jesus couldnt tell the difference if they was two nails. I was lookin forward t' givin you the little one.

SMILER *tosses half the cigarette onto the table. It rolls onto the floor.*

BARRY. Dont spoil my fag yer runt!

BARRY *kneels and gropes for the half cigarette under the table. He knocks over a chair. He gets it. Still kneeling, he lights it and inhales.*

BARRY. God I needed that.

BARRY *goes to the middle of the room to smoke in peace – as he inhales he bows his head to concentrate. SMILER puts the*

*other half cigarette back in the packet. He meticulously cleans
the blade and slips it in the packet behind the cigarettes. He
puts the packet in his shirt pocket. He takes a notebook from his
hip pocket and a pencil stub from behind his ear. He writes in
the notebook.*

SMILER. Put a sign on me nose when you're around:
trespassers will be prosecuted. Yer get right up it. Thass
fifty six an a 'arf.

Section Three – Mike's Cell

Day. MIKE *lies on one of the two beds. Through the open door a
prison officer is seen passing along the corridor outside. He is
followed by a prisoner pulling a trolley loaded with bundles of
dirty washing. Pause.* SMILER *passes by. A few seconds later
he comes back and leans on the wall opposite the open door. He
looks at* MIKE.

SMILER. They keep that face in a bin an 'and it round. Year
four. Yer look like snow thass bin pissed in just after they
made the thaw illegal.

A prisoner passes between SMILER *and the door.* SMILER
collars him.

SMILER. Three days! Out! Will yer miss me?
PRISONER (*friendly aggression*). Yer'll spent three bloody
years in 'ospital!

The prisoner goes.

SMILER (*to* MIKE). Come t' say cheerio.
MIKE. Monday . . .?

SMILER *levers himself off the wall and comes into the cell.
He half closes the door behind him.*

SMILER. Three days. If I last. Wont be time for cheerios

then. (*He sits on the other bed.*) 'Ave t' console the mob. What yer in for: frightenin ol' ladies with that mug? If you laughed yer'd go to the medic with a dangerous symptom.

MIKE *makes a friendly, tired gesture with his hand.*

SMILER. Ain so bad: four years then its down all the way. (*Hand gesture.*) The sunny side. I'll keep yer company for a bit. That all right? (*No answer.*) Dump eh? Architect put the rat 'oles in when they built it. That ol' crap-'eap get on yer nerves? If I let 'im 'e'd smoke the 'ole camel. Way beyond 'is means. I mix it with 'im so 'e keeps out a' real bother. Even a wimp like 'im can go the distance with the champ when its shadow boxin. Puts a bit a' shape in 'is life. 'E ain grateful. (*Slight pause.*) Thass it then. (*Suddenly stands and puts a finger to his lips.*) On Monday Im goin t' chuck all me ciggies in the air an let the lads scramble. Freebies!

SMILER *tiptoes to the door and suddenly opens it:* BARRY *comes in as if he's just arrived.*

SMILER. You're so bent your arse knows more words than your mouth.

SMILER *goes.*

BARRY. Watch it.

SMILER *goes away down the corridor.* BARRY *sits on the edge of his bed with the cigarette butt in his hand. He opens his locker and takes a pin from the shelf.*

BARRY. The little sod'll be back. Read 'is palm even if 'e was born with no arms. Give 'im a week. Six months at the most. (*He sticks the pin into the end of the butt.*) You dead? Make the most of it. The chaplain says it doesnt last. They come round and wake yer up. Dont suppose Smiler drop yer any ciggies? Might'a lashed out cause'a Monday. If 'e slashed an Jesus walked on the puddle 'e'd charge 'im for a ticket. Know where . . . (*He lights the stub and inhales.*) . . . 'is stash is. Dont finger it. Do it all verbal. Not mixin it with 'im an 'is mates – even if 'is ciggies was a mile long. Know what 'e's in for? 'E dont mind 'oo knows. Tell anyone for a packet a' twenty. No, tell *that* for nothin – only thing 'e dont charge for. (*He removes a shred of tobacco from his lip and examines it on the end of his finger.*) Carved 'is mate in a bar. Mate, mind – not an outsider. Cut 'is eye out. Not normal, like slashin a cheek. Made a proper job they say. Methodical. Talent for it. Would'a bin a surgeon if 'e'd come from a proper family. Poor ol' national 'ealth. (*He slides the shred of tobacco onto the smouldering butt. Inhales.*) Went for the other eye. Ambitious. Mates pulled 'im off. Bloke saw 'is own eye in the broken glass. 'Ad t' go somewhere. New meanin t' gazin in t' the crystal ball: Smiler's little joke when 'e tells it. Comes up every time. Know 'im from the cradle t' the gallows, as they used t' say. (*Small wince as he burns his lip.*) Wass 'e put in 'is fags? Fluff off a gorilla's groin. Think they're number one. The ocean couldnt dilute the piss they talk. (*Calls.*) Smiler! – See em in the visitors room. Their mothers an tarts. White faces. Starin great eyes. Like the eyes on those tree rats – or monkeys is it? – yer see on telly. (*Calls.*) Smiler! (– Watch me put 'im through 'is paces). In the visitors room. Then they give birth t' their kids. An yer see it in the kids. Even the little toddlers. Same little murderers' faces. Animals're descended from 'uman bein's. (*Calls.*) Oi! – You watch. Looks down on me cause a me 'abit. That ash's got more life in it than their kids.

BARRY *cleans the pin.* SMILER *comes in.*

SMILER. Three days! Three! Three! Three! (*He picks up a pillow and beats* BARRY *with it.*) Dont oi me yer git! Oi! Oi! Oi!
BARRY. Lay off yer bleedin nutter! Yer lost me pin!
SMILER. 'Oo you oi-in'? (*Chucks the pillow down.*) Im 'ere!
BARRY. Tell us what yer'll do on Monday Smiler.
SMILER. When they say on the news there's bin an earth

tremor thass me on the job. (BARRY *finds his pin*.) One day yer'll bend that pin an 'ave a twin.

BARRY *puts the pin on the shelf of his locker and shuts the door.*

BARRY. Yer'll be down the boozer too pissed 't get the wrinkles out.

SMILER. Mine dont 'ave wrinkles grandad. Thass where I notch up the virgins. Wass it worth? All the details before I sell it t' the press?

BARRY. Tell us Smiler. You're a lad. Slip it in eh?

SMILER. Yer lecherous ol' lag! (*Yells.*) Three days! (*To* BARRY.) Forty ciggies on account?

PRISONER 1 (*off*). Put a sock in it Smiler!

PRISONER 2 (*off*). Yer sayin yer prayers?

PRISONER 1 (*off*). Pullin me plonker! Show some respect for the workin man!

SMILER (*to* BARRY). Get 'ard on it t'night? Yer couldnt get 'ard if they give yer an iron spike an cement injections. No Im not tellin you. Ain wasted time in 'ere – I learnt. Not the garbage they feed yer. I watched the lot that put us 'ere – thass where I learnt. They're the crooks – an they get away with it. They can't fail. Its their set-up – all that out there: the rich man's racket. From now on its number one. I give that poxy shower enough a' my life. Aint comin back next time. (*Yells.*) Three days! (*Off, groans. He yells.*) Out! Screwin boozin cars Costa Brava lolly!

PRISONER 2 (*off*). Thank chriss! Then we'll get a bit a' shut-eye!

BARRY. You're a lad Smiler. Slip it in eh? Tell us.

SMILER (*suddenly still*). I cant. I told yer. Screwin boozin cars trip-t'-the-sea lolly: 's foreign language in 'ere. Yer cant understand nothin in 'ere. I only know what it means cause the door's openin for out. If I tried t' tell yer its like writin on a sheet a' paper an' the words come out on the other side: all you see's blank, 's out there where it means.

BARRY. Six months. You'll be back.

SMILER (*very still*). Yer see? Yer cant understand. Givvus

givvus givvus: its freedom innit? (*Jumps up and yells.*)
What sod said put a sock in it?

SMILER *runs out. Off, prisoners' yells and shouts of 'Shuttit
nutter!'*

Section Four – Association Area – Cupboard – Washroom, Prison Yard – Mike's Cell

MIKE *holding a rope. It has been made by tying two ropes
together. Low electric light. MIKE is standing in a cupboard.
The cupboard is the blocked-off part of a corridor. Longish and
darkish. Near the top along one side there is a shelf backed by a
wooden plank. Pipes on the walls and ceilings. Mops, squeegees,
floor-cloths, blocks of industrial soap and buckets with mop-grills
in the top – one bucket stands under a tap in a corner. Two
domestic chairs, one inverted with its seat on the seat of the other.*

MIKE *takes down the top chair and wedges its back under the
door handle. He stands the other chair under a pipe that crosses
the ceiling. He begins to tie the end of the rope into a noose. He is
weak and sits on the chair to finish it. He climbs onto the chair.
From a trouser side-pocket he takes a small envelope – blue,
crinkled, with worn edges. He props it against the plank behind
the shelf.*

*He passes the end of the rope over the pipe on the ceiling and knots
it. For a moment he stands in silence. His hand strays to his side
in the gesture of a child that wants to wee. He steps down from the
chair – and this moves it so that it is no longer directly under the
noose. He takes away the chair wedging the door and opens it.*

MIKE *closes the cupboard door behind him. No one else is
about. The camera follows him as he crosses the Association Area
and goes down the corridor till he comes to the washroom.*

*He crosses the washroom, passes the urinals and goes out of sight
into a cubicle. He doesnt close the door. Pause. The toilet is
flushed. MIKE comes out of the cubicle, crosses the washroom,
goes into the corridor and along it till he reaches a window.*

MIKE *looks down into the yard from the second storey. Dusk. The yard is surrounded by security fencing and lit by security lights. On the far side of the yard there is a long one-storey utility hut with a row of brightly lit windows in the wall facing the yard.*

It is after office hours but in one window a warder crosses with some files. He wears a shirt with rolled-up sleeves and a tie. He crouches, opens the bottom drawer in a desk, puts the files into it and closes it. He goes away.

MIKE's *hand gently brushes the pane – a gesture like a segment of a handwave.*

In one movement he turns and continues calmly along the corridor. He reaches the Association Area. He crosses it and goes to the cupboard.

Still calm he puts his hand on the door handle and opens the door.

SMILER *is hanging in the noose.*

A chair lies on its side under the body. The other chair is where MIKE *had left it.* MIKE *runs into the cupboard. He tries to support the body and loosen the noose. He cant. The body swings round, twisting away from him as if its fighting him.* MIKE *whimpers and tries to support it and hook the chair towards him with his foot but his foot pushes it further away. He lets the body swing, picks up the chair, stands it by the body and climbs onto it. He tugs the body towards him. The legs flop against the chair – it almost topples. He hitches the weight of the body off the rope and loosens it. He drags it over the face, squashing and grazing the nose and cheeks and yanking open the mouth. He stands on the chair holding the body and breathes into its mouth. He climbs down. The chair lurches from under him, crashes into the wall and bounces away. He stumbles to the ground with the body and falls on top of it. He shakes it.*

MIKE. Smiler. Smiler. No. No. (*Stands, lost, blank.*) I – where is the – ? What 'ave – ? (*Looks down at the body. Slowly he kneels by the body, hits the chest, breathes into the mouth.*) Please.

MIKE *stands. Looks round, sees the chair, picks it up, puts it under the noose and starts to climb onto it: one leg tangles with the body, the foot of the leg pressed into its hand.*

MIKE. No! No! Let go! Give me the chair! I will! I will!

MIKE *savagely kicks the body away – the chair is free. He climbs onto it and reaches for the noose. It is much larger than it was – stretched when it was pulled from the head. MIKE holds the bottom of the noose with both hands and pulls it open so that it forms a perfect equilateral triangle. He holds the bottom straight and pulls down to keep the triangle rigid. He puts his head into it. He feels with his foot to kick the chair away.*

MIKE's *head, hands and the rope triangle. His hands grip the bottom of the triangle as if it were a rail. Pause. Suddenly his face cracks – it seems to burst into pieces – and water pours from his eyes and the cracks as if his face were breaking up and washing away in a flood. Dribble spills from his mouth. He makes a sound. Slowly he lets go of the rope, creeps down from the chair, huddles against a wall and cries. He runs out of the cupboard.*

MIKE *runs.*

MIKE. Help! Help! Help! You bastards! 'E's dyin!

There is a moment before two prisoners come into the corridor. MIKE turns to run back.

MIKE *is kneeling by the body breathing into its mouth.*

Two Prison Officers come into the cupboard.

MIKE. 'E pulled the chair when I stood on the –
PRISON OFFICER 1. Out!
MIKE. 'E's alive!
PRISON OFFICER 2. Out! Out! Out!

PRISON OFFICER 2 *pulls* MIKE *from the body and throws him from the cupboard.* PRISON OFFICER 1 *bends over the body and gives expert resuscitation treatment. Through the open door* MIKE *is partly seen getting to his feet in the Association Area.* PRISON OFFICER 3 *appears behind him, jumps round him, comes to the cupboard door and looks in. He says nothing. Other prisoners come into the Association Area and come toward the cupboard. MIKE stands with his head bowed.*

PRISON OFFICER 2 (*low*). Get that shower out.
PRISON OFFICER 3 (*turning*). Cells! Cells! Cells!

PRISON OFFICER 2 *slams the door in the prisoners' faces. They try to open it.*

PRISON OFFICER 3, MIKE, *prisoners.*

PRISON OFFICER 3. Move!
PRISONER 1. Whass up?
PRISONER 2. 'Oo they got?
PRISONER 3. 'Oo's on the floor?

PRISON OFFICER 4 *comes into the Association Area. He bangs on the cupboard door.*

PRISON OFFICER 4 (*calls*). 'S Jenks! (*The door is opened slightly. He looks in.*) Chriss.

PRISON OFFICER 4 *helps* PRISON OFFICER 3 *to clear the Association Area.*

PRISON OFFICER 4. Move! Let's 'ave yer!
PRISONER 3. Dont bloody push! 'Oo they got?
PRISON OFFICER 3. Move! Nothin t' see!

Corridor.

MIKE, *other prisoners,* PRISON OFFICER 3 and PRISON OFFICER 4. *Hassle. An alarm starts. MIKE stalks through the others like a zombie.*

PRISONERS. Bastards! Bastards! 'Oo they got! What they up to? Dont want no witnesses!
PRISON OFFICER 3. Move or there'll be trouble!
PRISONER 2 (*to MIKE*). Yer said dyin!

MIKE *doesnt respond.*

PRISONER 3. 'S a rope!

PRISONER 4 (*calls*). Rope!
PRISONERS. Its rope! Rope! Rope! Another one!
PRISON OFFICER 4. Not a rope!
PRISONERS. Rope!
PRISONER 4. A massacre!
PRISON OFFICER 3. Accident!
PRISON OFFICER 4. Yer'd queue t' see an empty piss pot!

The prisoners shout as the prison officers hustle them to the cells.

MIKE's cell.

Electric light. Door shut. Off, the alarm, doors banging, feet and shouts: 'Rope! Another one! Bastards! Move!'

MIKE half-sits, half-crouches on his bed with his face to the wall and gasps as if he's run round the world. His hand slides along the wall, and then he levers himself off it and slowly, still crying – without fuss, like a mechanical toy – crawls off the bunk, creeps under it and goes out of sight.

Inside the cupboard.

PRISON OFFICER 1 and PRISON OFFICER 2 with the body. PRISON OFFICER 3 and PRISON OFFICER 5 in the open doorway.

PRISON OFFICER 1 (*interrupts his resuscitation for a moment*). Kill that bloody racket. Its not wakin 'im up an its givin me an earache.
PRISON OFFICER 2. Would choose the end a shift!

PRISON OFFICER 1 looks up – his expression changes. He sees BARRY's head peering over the backs of PRISON OFFICER 3 and PRISON OFFICER 5.

PRISON OFFICER 1. 'Op it scrag!

PRISON OFFICER 3 spins round and frog-marches BARRY away.

MIKE's cell.

As before but seemingly empty. Off, the alarm – it stops

abruptly and MIKE's *sobbing is heard: a brief downward scale. The shot is brief.*

MIKE (*unseen*). Uh – uh – uh – uh – uh.

Inside the cupboard.

PRISON OFFICER 1, PRISON OFFICER 2 *and* PRISON OFFICER 5 *and the body.* PRISON OFFICER 1 *stops resuscitation.*

PRISON OFFICER 1. 'E 's gone to the great prison in the sky.

PRISON OFFICER 2 *sees the envelope on the shelf. He takes it down.*

PRISON OFFICER 2. Remembered t' post early for Chrissmass. Shall I . . . ?

PRISON OFFICER 5. Its 'is thankyou letter.

PRISON OFFICER 1 *takes the envelope and opens it.*

PRISON OFFICER 1. Might've left a forwardin' address . . . (*Takes out a note and sees the signature.*) No 'e aint.

Section Five – Mike's Cell

Day. BARRY *and* MIKE *alone.* BARRY *sits on the bed with an open cardboard suitcase on it in front of him. In the suitcase, assorted packets of about eight hundred cigarettes. A few more packets on the bed beside the case.*

BARRY (*looking at the packets*). Could'a left 'im me pin in me will. (*Looks up at* MIKE.) Know where 'e 'ad it 'id? That cupboard. Be'ind the board on the shelf. Not some little bog 'ole. Move arf the wall t' get at it. Smart.

MIKE *takes no notice of* BARRY. *He stands close to the window looking at it. A noise at the door.* BARRY *quickly and neatly drops a blanket over the case and the loose packets.*

The door opens slightly and a uniformed arm comes through and beckons.

PRISON OFFICER 2 (*off*). Visitor.

Section Six – Probation Office
'Four Lumps of Sugar'

Day. A small room with a desk. Behind the desk an office chair and in front of it a visitors chair with padded back and pads on bent wood arms. On the desk a lamp, a typewriter, empty office trays and two cups of coffee. Four sugar lumps on the desk beside the cups. A wastepaper basket. Wall charts, lists, rosters, holiday postcards, etc.

ELLEN, SMILER's mother, stands at the desk. She is in her forties and has longish hair. She wears a street coat. She is making an effort to control her grief. MIKE sits in the visitors chair.

ELLEN. I said I didnt want to go in the visitors room. The Probation Officer said we could use his office for half an hour. He was nice about it. I cant understand what happened.

MIKE. There'll be an inquest.

ELLEN. The Probation Officer said you were the last one to speak to him.

MIKE. No 'e was dead when I got there.

ELLEN. Two days. He'd've been out. His room was ready. We were going to celebrate. I know what he'd done was bad. It would've been different – he'd grown out of it. But they put them in these places. Like living on the edge of the cliff. They make them worse.

MIKE. Everyone liked 'im.

ELLEN (*she sits*). Why did he do it?

MIKE. Im sorry.

ELLEN. You gave him the rope. The Probation Officer –

MIKE. I cant 'elp yer missus.

ELLEN. If you hadnt given him the rope he couldnt have done it.

MIKE stands to go.

ELLEN. You must've passed him in the corridor? I dont care what it is. Tell me. They smile or they're busy and shout at you. Now you! I thought if I spoke to someone inside . . . Didnt you see he was in trouble? Everyone liked him? They didnt like him very much if they let this happen. And who are you to like my son? You're criminals – half animals – not boys like him. If you could like anyone you wouldnt be in these places! . . . If he'd come out for a few days – then been run over! – he'd've had something. You had years before you came here. He had nothing. I want to know what happened!

MIKE. I tied the rope. Its quiet in the evening. 'Our before they lock us up. I wouldnt be found too soon. They just 'ad t' get rid of what's left. These places can handle that. Part a' the routine. Few extra forms.

ELLEN. You left the rope there?

MIKE. When I'd worked out what t' do I shut off. Kept my mind blank. Went round like a zombie. Didnt think – in case I lost me nerve. Then when it was all ready – I realised I wanted t' pee. I'd even shut that out. All day. They say when yer 'ang yer lose control. I didnt want t' be found like a baby wettin itself. At least I'd learned somethin while I was alive.

ELLEN. You wanted to pee so he . . . ?

MIKE. . . . Screws laughin . . . detail a lad t' mop up . . . didnt want that. I was away three minutes. The shock of findin the rope . . . must've bin the last straw . . . ?

ELLEN. It was a joke. He found the rope – knew it was you because he saw you leave – and you said you were fond of him – so he wanted to joke you out of it. Everything was a joke to him! He stood on the chair – when the door opened – he was excited – so he slipped . . .

MIKE. 'E was dead when I got back.

ELLEN. In three minutes? He found the rope and did it in three minutes!

MIKE. It coulda bin four or five. I didnt look at the watch. There'll be an inquest.

ELLEN. What good's that to me? They didnt find out why he was alive at his trial, why should they bother to find out why he's dead at an inquest? Im the only one who wants to know the truth. He wasnt anybody. They'll blame him because its easiest. They'd've lent him a rope! I want to know why! . . . I wont let you down. I wouldnt tell them if they *were* interested. They're nothing. I cant live through the rest of my life with it preying on my mind. If I'd nursed him. I didnt even say good-bye. See you on Monday its a date.

MIKE. 'E was scared.

ELLEN. You mean the other lad? No no even he said it could've been the other way round – he could've hurt my son. He didnt hold a grudge. Sit down. Your coffee's getting cold. Perhaps you'll think of something you forgot in all the upset. Or someone's said something since?

MIKE *looks at his watch and sits.*

ELLEN. I used to pass the empty prams by the wall. Smelt of milk and washing. Empty baby straps. Nappies squashed up in plastic bags. Even the devil'd cry here. He died here. Like climbing down into a grave to hang yourself. (*Pause.*) Well I certainly came on a fool's errand. I suppose they dont let you out of their sight.

MIKE. I shant try it again.

ELLEN. No. You wouldnt. Had a chance to see. Put on a show. What did he look like on the end of a rope? Tell me. Then the journey's not wasted. Did he have time to pee? (*Silence.*) You look the sort that makes other people do your suffering for you. Your face is like a mincer with sympathy coming through. Yes you keep quiet. I'll find out. You'll pay. I wont bother with their trials and tribunals. There must be somewhere to turn for – I'll make my own justice! God this is a rotten world. I hope you hang. Open a cupboard and there's the rope! You should be dead. He's here but you're stood in front of him. You cant change everything: I'd've smiled at him – I hate you! Get out of his chair!

MIKE *stands abruptly: the empty chair.*

O he's dead. Sit. Sit. Sit in his chair. (MIKE *sits.*) Rather my enemy than that emptiness. I know what he did, but he was good. I want him back.

MIKE. I cant 'elp.

ELLEN (*order*). Sit there. It helps. (*Pause. Slow with hatred.*) You look at your watch? I'll tell you when its time. You took his life, you can give me half an hour. You're breathing his air – everything you do now's a swindle. I'll hate you when Im dying. Look forward to it. No distractions then, shopping, catching the bus, all the little things you have to do to stay alive . . . just you, to hate. Lie in my bed and hate. Im glad I came. My pulse is hammering away. D'you take sugar? (*Puts the four sugar lumps one by one in her coffee.*) I dont take it. But you're not having it. (*Stirs coffee.*) A little practice in hate. (*Sips.*) Muck. (*Puts the cup down.*) I forgot you're fed on swill. Can I ask you a question? (*No answer.*) How long you in for?

MIKE. Life.

Silence. She gives a short sharp giggle.

(*Quietly.*) Im sorry your son died. This is the pits, really. The morgue where they put the living. Me – 'im – some other number – oo's it matter 'oo used the rope? I could be dead. Out a' this. I should'a done it when I found 'im. 'E wouldnt a' minded about the piss. Let the screws laugh. Now I cant. Cant get the courage up twice. 'E stole my rope. If 'e was a cannibal 'e'd steal off 'is neighbour's plate. I dont know what was wrong between yer. Dont take it out on me. Dont cry – I seen through that. See through too much in 'ere. When they lower me in my grave I'll be starin in t' my tears on the bottom.

ELLEN (*absently*). He changed in here. He wouldnt tell me. After a while I dont think 'e knew me unless I told him my name.

MIKE (*fumbles with a piece of paper*). My suicide note. (*Holds it out to her.*) Might be some use. (*She doesnt take it.*) It'll be read at the inquest.

ELLEN *reads the note as he holds it in his hand.*

MIKE. A copy. Wouldnt give me the original. Thass the property a' the court.

Section Seven – Mike's Cell

Day. MIKE lies on the only bed. On a shelf beside it there is a mug of tea with a spoon in it. Without looking at what he does he takes the mug from the shelf. He holds the spoon for a moment. He begins to stir the tea.

Section Eight – Visiting Room in an Open Prison

Day. Prisoners and visitors sit at separate tables and drink coffee, tea and fruit juice. Some of the adults nurse infants and older children on their knees. Other children stand and stare or wander or play with prison toys. A Prison Officer.

MIKE stands at his table and looks towards the door. VERA has just sat. She wears a brown coat and a loose pale knitted-string beret.

VERA. Arent you excited?

MIKE. Yer said Frank was coming.

VERA. Outside, being tactful. Sit down.

MIKE. Whass 'e want?

VERA. Didnt bring anything. Only extra to carry out. You dont want to leave anything behind. He hasnt said.

MIKE *sits.*

VERA. Hardly seen him since he sold me your flat. Found

him on the front door in his uniform. I knew he joined the police when he moved. I thought: panic – he wants the flat back! The thoughts go through your head. The flat's mine. He cant touch it. Payments up to date. He wanted me to ask you to send him a visiting order. Suppose he wouldnt write to you in case you said no. They train the police in social work now. He'll offer to stand by you, say he doesnt hold a grudge. Ask me, he owes *you*: you *gave* him the flat. He certainly didnt think of that when he sold it to me!

A child wandering with a glass of orange juice leans on her knee and offers her the glass. Without looking at it she steers it away.

VERA. There's a luvvy go to mummy. – Cant wait to see your face when you see the flat. All new – even the – ! No you'll see it for yourself! I had to struggle. You're worth it. (*She is going to pat his hand but doesnt.*) This isnt the place for emotions. Frank'll know what to do if you get into trouble.

MIKE. I wont get into trouble.

VERA. We wont let you. As long as you dont get upset and dont try to do everything yourself. Its all changed. Ten years is what ten lifetimes used to be. A day or two's rest, then we'll look for a job. Wont rush it. Two to keep, and the mortgage. You wont believe the prices. Frank brought me in the car. I'd love to know what he's after. I'll pop out and send him in. Make a note of everything he says. He might drop little hints you dont understand. All right?

VERA *stands and goes towards the door.* MIKE *watches her. At the door she turns to mouth, emphasizing the words with stabs of her index finger: 'Dont worry – it'll be all right – I'll be back soon.'*

MIKE *stares at the door when she has gone. The wandering child comes to his table and plays sliding its glass of orange juice on the table top.* MIKE *doesnt notice.*

CHILD. Brr. Brr.

FRANK *enters. He is in civvies: a white woollen polo-neck sweater, dark trousers and shoes and a light brown hound's-tooth tweed jacket with a folded newspaper in a pocket. MIKE stands as FRANK comes towards him and holds out his hand. FRANK stops before he reaches MIKE's table.*

MIKE. Frank. Thanks for giving Vera a lift. (FRANK *hasnt taken his hand.* MIKE *hesitates.*) The flat seems to have kept her busy. (*No answer.*) Policeman must feel funny visiting 'is pal in prison.

FRANK *speaks in a low voice, but naturally so that it doesnt attract attention.*

FRANK. You bastard. That's all.

CHILD (*sliding the glass on the table*). Brr. Brr.

FRANK *turns and walks away.* MIKE *stares after him. The child spills orange on the table top and writes in it with a finger. Three-quarters of the way across the room* FRANK *turns and comes back.* MIKE *realises now that he is white with anger.*

CHILD. Slop. Slop.

FRANK (*as before, but now as if his mouth is almost paralysed with anger*). You shouldnt be – all you should be hanged – pollute the streets. You see me – first word: flat. You didnt buy me. Duty.

The child turns to FRANK *and with one hand pulls at his trousers and with the other offers him the glass of orange juice.* FRANK *doesnt notice it.*

FRANK. Im glad I saw you – your box.

CHILD'S MOTHER (*off*). Dont wet the gentleman's trousers Dilly.

FRANK. You're not out – your time starts. You're tied to my eyeballs.

The child's mother comes and gathers it away without noticing FRANK's *anger.*

FRANK. You look forward – hands on innocent people.
Your first move its your last.

*FRANK goes. MIKE stares after him with a blank face. The
spilt orange juice glistens on the table.*

PART THREE

Section One – The Flat – Living Room

VERA *has 'modernized'* MIKE's *old flat with new furniture, carpets, covers, wallpapers, lights, ornaments and objets de kitsch. The flat is small and over-crowded but the triviality of the things over-crowding it make it seem empty.*

MIKE *is in a chair at the table.* VERA *is at the sideboard. She picks up a tray on which are a sherry decanter, two glasses and a glass bowl of nuts and raisins.*

VERA. The look on your face! You didn't expect all this! All the changes are mine. Frank only tinkered when he had it. Sit in an armchair.

MIKE. Im all right.

VERA (*points*). You had your table there. I put mine so you can see the street. (*Remembers.*) O! (*She goes to the stereo and plays a James Last CD.*) Too late to play it loud. You can hear the volume t'morrow. (*Sherry toast.*) To us.

MIKE. Us.

VERA. Want a bite to eat?

MIKE. No.

VERA. You're tired.

MIKE. No.

VERA. The long journey. We should go to bed when you're ready.

VERA *goes out through the hall door. From time to time* MIKE's *eyes flicker round the room.*

VERA (*off*). Im nervous.

MIKE. Why did you want t' live 'ere. Yer could-a moved out.

VERA (*off*). You've got a perfect right to be in that room. Anyway – a single woman – it was all I could afford. No removal van. Two lads downstairs carried it all up. I only set out to change the furniture but you could see the marks in the pile where yours had stood. So I got a new carpet. Its all paid for – except the mortgage. The bank statement tells me where I am every month. (*Slight pause.*) *You murdered your daughter and spent ten years in prison.* That doesnt make you worse in my eyes. You suffered so you're bound to feel nibbled round the edges. Makes you appreciate what we've got! No use blaming the past if we do wrong now. You've got to have good thoughts – learn to accept responsibilities again.

VERA *comes in wearing a nightgown, a quilted dressing-gown and mandarin slippers.*

VERA. That's the first time you've been in this room since it happened. Left you alone on purpose. You feel better now you've faced it.

MIKE *goes to an armchair and sits.*

VERA. You do like it?

MIKE *raises his eyebrows, compresses his lips and shakes his head to show his admiration.*

VERA. There's lots more sherry. You're not worried about living in sin? Be modern for a bit! You're here that's the main thing. You'll soon be proposing. (*Gesture.*) All this – the extra stability – your probation officer'd be pleased. If you go wrong this time you'll be in for good – it wont be a long weekend.

MIKE. I might sit 'ere t'night.

VERA. I understand. Let me fetch you a blanket.

MIKE. There was a lad inside. Only young. 'E was due out in two days: 'e anged 'isself. I thought about it all those years. I was goin' t' serve my time quietly – then two days before the end do a runner: escape. I even 'oped – cause I'd taken the risk – I'd find out why 'e'd done it. Why all the other things. It'd come t' me while I was runnin. Then Frank came – an put the fear a' god in me. Dont suppose I'd'a done it anyway. No guts. I cant now: ten years down the drain. I dont know 'ow t' live. I don't know what t' do.

VERA. Thank god for Frank! If you'd done that they'd've put you in Broadmoor for life.

MIKE. I didnt murder Sheila.

VERA. You're not going to start all that Mike? I thought we'd got over it. You know it frightens me. O! – dont let me forget: your key.

MIKE. I didnt murder her.

VERA. You told the judge you did! Everything's been so nice. Dont spoil our first night. (*Gestures round.*) Im sorry its nothing better. If you hadnt gone to prison you'd have somewhere much nicer by now. You're a hard worker. You'd've taken advantage of all the new opportunities. Or found yourself a good-looker with money. You missed out once, dont miss out again. We deserve our bit of happiness.

VERA goes out and comes back with a blanket. She covers MIKE and kneels beside him.

VERA. Warm? I dont expect I make the most of myself. (*Rests her head on his lap.*) T' tell the truth I let myself go. Didnt have the time. Now you're here I'll get rid of the strain. (*Laugh.*) T'morrow I'll be ten years younger. Or you'll be running after some fancy pair of legs. No more silly talk. We havent got the time.

MIKE. Did yer choose it all yerself? – all the colours.

VERA. There you are! See how nice you can be! I knew you'd have a little crisis. Now its over. (*Strokes the back of his hand.*) You try to understand too much, instead of looking for the way out – like the rest of us. It was bound to go wrong. You don't want this silly old blanket?

No response. VERA goes out and comes back with another blanket.

VERA. Not leaving you alone t'night. I know the signs. (*She sits in the other armchair and covers herself with the blanket.*) Frank'll be your guardian angel.

MIKE. I didnt do it.

VERA. That's enough Mike.

MIKE. I cant 'elp it. Thass got t' be the basis from now on.

VERA (*sudden anger*). Its not right to play me up! Are you

going to appeal? Whose money? You're not throwing my savings down the drain. Get up a petition for the flats? They wanted you to hang. You'll be the laughing stock. Turn into some old crank going round in slippers with a billboard on his back 'I never did it!' Never heard such rot! Look at this carpet. In that cupboard there's a set of these glasses for when we have people in. You're not to sit there and smash the home for me! Its always number one! (*Calmer.*) Sorry Im on edge. Im the one entitled to be over-wrought. You havent said one nice thing about all my work. I ask you if you like it and you pull a funny face. Now your blanket! Worse than a child! Cant even keep a blanket on! (*She wraps his blanket closer around him.*) Someone did it. You'd still've lost a daughter. Everything would've changed. Let's stop it Mike (*She folds up her blanket.*) Come to bed. We'll just go to sleep. Or lie there. At least we'll be each other's company. Its not easy to get back into life. They gave you a booklet. The longer you put it off the harder it is. Do it for the –

MIKE. Stop it! Stop it! . . . I dont care about the flats! Its not even the prison! And god knows I cant bring Sheila back! I want t' tell the truth in my own 'ouse. You sit there an tell me Im a monster an then say get back t' normal! Whass normal? – murder? I didnt do it.

VERA. You did.

MIKE. Im sorry. This isnt what you planned.

VERA. O I knew you'd have this row. Been looking forward to it! I didnt call you monster. I dont know why you cant *say* it. You did it – is saying it worse? You killed her.

MIKE. I didnt! Men dont do that!

VERA. They do!

MIKE. Where's my jacket?

MIKE *goes into the kitchen.* VERA *stands.*

VERA. You're going out. You cant. You havent got a key. I'll ring the probation. They left an emergency number.

MIKE *comes back.*

MIKE. I cant live 'ere. Yer put me jacket somewhere.

MIKE *goes towards the hall.*

MIKE's *small suitcase stands flat against a wall.*

VERA *overtakes* MIKE *in the hall and blocks the front door.*

VERA. Please. Please. Nothing's the matter. You dont like the furniture. We'll change it. You can do that nowadays. Let me get you a warmer blanket. Tell me what you want. I've got money if you need it. Is it your own room? Sleep alone. You be in charge. That's what I want. I *want*! Im tired of doing all the thinking. You decide. Please Mike. Dont leave me.

MIKE *turns and goes back towards the living room.* VERA *follows* MIKE *in.*

VERA. They catch you in the streets at night without a jacket they'll put you away. You made your point Mike. You win. I wont say another word. I wont even tell them if you hit me. (*She takes his jacket from the seat of a chair and gives it to him.*) There's your jacket. I'll have to sew that tear before it gets any bigger. I wanted it to go so well. My fault. Im such a silly cow. I go on and all you need is rest. We're both tired. What d'you want me to think? Im the sort of woman a man runs away from the first night after ten years? I know its true but dont do it to me. You cant ask me to live with that. I waited so long. It doesn't matter if it hurts you. Stay. Think of me for once.

MIKE. Yer knew I wouldnt stay. Its obvious – yer can think out 'ere. Inside yer kid yerself about everythin.

VERA *sits sideways in the armchair, drawing up her legs so that she seems to crouch, facing away from him.*

VERA. Dont go. Dont go.

MIKE. Its a shock because its finished so soon. Yer thought yer could draw it out for weeks – months – go through all the details. Yer need that. I cant. Sheila could've bin in that chair all these years. Waitin t' be told I didnt do it. She wants a good man for 'er father. I didnt kill 'er.

VERA (*crouches as before*). I dont understand when you talk like that. You need your ideas. That's why I love you. But you have to live in our world. Someone must wash and cook for you. They did it for you in prison. I could do it for you. My hands feel grubby when I touch you. Show me the other things. I want to know. But dont go. Please. Please.

MIKE. Its best. Im a fool, I –

VERA (*curls tighter still facing away from him*). Other people are happy. Why cant I be? O please. (*Cries.*)

MIKE (*putting on his jacket*). I'll take my things. You neednt see me again. I'll always say I didnt do it. That's no use t' you. You wish I did.

VERA *falls out of the chair to his feet. She grabs the ends of his trousers and squeezes them into two fistfuls.*

VERA. Dont leave me. Dont leave me. Please. I dont understand. I'll go out of my mind. I hate this place! Hate it! (*She bites a fistful of trouser.*) Hu – hu – hu – hu. Hate it. Hate it. Hate it. Or kill me – and let me get out that way.

MIKE *helps her to her feet.*

VERA. Yes. Yes. That's better. So kind. (*Wipes her face with her hand.*) So kind. Scaring me. There's no one like you in the world. Give me your case. Wait till morning. Then you can – . O god you make me sound like your gaoler. You'll wait till I sleep and then escape. I've got to sleep – cant stay awake all my life. (*Dabs her eyes with her hands.*) You could walk out next week. Anytime. Doors are everywhere. I'll never trust you now. Doors, doors. There's nothing I can do. (*She sits on the edge of the armchair seat, facing away from him. Talks almost automatically.*) Someone – I heard them on the stair – you said – the police confuse you – strangers come in as they like – because the area – the flats are poor – no they'd've stopped her in the entrance – unless they wanted money – and came up with her to the . . . someone . . .

MIKE *sits on an arm of* VERA's *chair. He faces away from*

her, leaning his elbows on his knees so that his hands hang in space.

MIKE. I've bin angry for ten years. Five prisons. Cant think inside. *She's* not sittin there. They ground 'er up long ago. Im not angry. Its the sky. Not used t' it. I killed 'er: but I didnt. 'Ow can I answer that?

VERA. I wish I'd killed her. Another woman's jealousy. I could tell you you didnt do it. I'd be so happy. I hope she's in hell. The little bitch. She made me suffer.

MIKE. I'd better go.

VERA (*whispering to herself*). Ten years . . . in prison every day. Get up. Work. Save every penny. I couldnt afford to look at other people's faces. They were happy. The faces would've been a knife in me. (*She clenches her fist and presses the side of her index finger against her teeth.*) I've given my life up for today. That's what it cost me: you standing there. Its not murder. When you murdered her you paid. You murder me and I pay. She sent you – all those years ago – you've only just found what she wanted. You murdered the wrong one. It should've been me. You're evil – that's why you're always asking for the truth. (*She puts her hand in the pocket of her dressing gown. She takes out a little ring of keys and throws it on the floor.*) I locked the front door when I got ready for the night. Anyone who lies down next to you's already in their grave. You used to be a weak little man. I shouldnt be surprised if you had periods. You're changed. I dont want you here.

MIKE. Per'aps later – if I –

VERA. No. Take your filth away. (*With her foot she straightens a ruck she made in the carpet when she was on the floor.*) Dont want your dust and dirt and smut. This place is sacred. All of you stay out. (*She straightens the carpet with her hand.*) You're all murderers making excuses. I'll keep this place holy. Talk to myself. My mother used to sing to me. Play my CDs. Its in my name.

There is water in her eyes but she doesnt cry. Mike picks up the keys. He goes out with his case.

Section Two – Ellen's House – Front Doorstep – Hall – Living-Room
'Two Shoes'

Night. The front door opens. ELLEN *stands there. She raises her eyes to* MIKE's *face.*

MIKE. You dont remember me.

    ELLEN *closes the door a fraction.*

In prison.
ELLEN. What d'you want?
MIKE. I come out t'day.
ELLEN. Its late.
MIKE. About your son.
ELLEN (*hesitates*). Come back t'morrow.
MIKE. I 'ave t' go away.

    ELLEN *thinks for a moment.*

    ELLEN's *living room.*

    The room is about the size of Vera's but is comfortable, with simple furniture and decoration.

    MIKE *and* ELLEN *stand looking at each other. He holds his case.*

MIKE. I couldn't stay at home.
ELLEN. You want to tell me something about my son?
MIKE. Can I sit? (*He remains standing.*)
ELLEN. You haven't got anything to tell me. Go. I cant talk about him. He's been dead six years. (*She moves towards the hall door.*)
MIKE. I tied the rope to 'ang meself. 'E found it and 'anged 'isself. (*Confused.*) I should be dead. Your son give me my life – or 'is – or I took it –
ELLEN. You didn't kill him?
MIKE. No.
ELLEN. Please go. I shouldnt've let you in. I cant help you. He mixed me up in trials and inquests and wounds – I dont

understand those things. I go to work, do the shopping, get on with life. I've forgotten him.

MIKE. I murdered my daughter. We rowed about a teacup. You dont murder over that. I loved 'er. I thought about it for ten years. I wanted it t' go slower so I could think. There was just three words: Im innocent. They joke when they're comin out: swillin, screwin. They dont believe it. They kill – or break somethin – t' go back in. If they dont its no different: there isnt any 'out'. Your son knew, 'e mastered that. 'E killed 'isself when 'e was comin out. If I knew why, I'd know all the rest. I'd'a put a piece a' chalk in 'is 'and so 'e could scrawl it on the prison wall while 'e was swingin. Inside they're cruel an' stupid: but I can respect them. They are what they are. Out 'ere people are like beetles under stones: only they live under other people. 'Ow can I live out 'ere? I dont know what t' do.

ELLEN. You must go.

MIKE (*he sits on his case*). I spent me money on a taxi. Didnt want t' be too late. If Im found wanderin . . . conditional release. Used t' little rooms. The streets scare me. (*Glances round.*) There's no photo of 'im.

ELLEN. Sleep in the chair. You'll have to leave when I do – I go to work in the morning.

MIKE (*sits in the armchair*). Per'aps between us we could think . . . ?

ELLEN. I lay awake for years. There's nothing. I wish you hadnt come. Its not fair.

A doorbell: three short rings – ELLEN *looks up in surprise. The front door is heard opening and slamming.* OLIVER *comes in. He has been drinking but is not drunk. He is twenty-six, stocky, with greasy dark hair and is dressed in a dark suit, a white shirt unbuttoned at the collar and no tie. He has one eye.*

OLIVER. Company! (*Pecks* ELLEN.) 'Ad a party?

OLIVER *flops into an armchair and leans back with his legs spread. He raises his hand in Indian Chief greeting to* MIKE.

OLIVER. Hi. Olly.

MIKE. Mike.

OLIVER (*mimes shaking hands across the distance*). Please t' meet yer.

OLIVER *eases off his shoes with his feet.*

ELLEN (*to* OLIVER). We used to know each other.

OLIVER. 'Ad a take-away in the street. (MIKE's *case.*) Goin far?

MIKE. I was lookin for a place. Somewhere cheap local.

OLIVER. Let 'er put yer up. Got plenty a' room.

ELLEN. Nowhere's made up.

OLIVER. That chair!

MIKE (*stands*). Dont want t' be a –

OLIVER. Suit yerself. (*Bends forwards, picks up his shoes and tosses them behind his armchair.*) Wont get nowhere local this time a' night. (*No answer.*) If no one else is puttin the kettle on . . .

OLIVER *goes into the kitchen. Sounds of kettle, water, etc.*

ELLEN. He'll stay for a week or so. Turns up when his drinking's got him in a state. Then he's off for months. He's the one my son – destroyed his eye. (*Shrug.*) I let him use his old room.

Section Three – The Same
'The Empty Vase'

The next afternoon. MIKE *sits at the table. His jacket is on the back of his chair. He wears a sleeveless pullover.* OLIVER *comes through the kitchen door. He wears slacks, sweatshirt and a crumpled baseball cap.*

OLIVER. Stoppin'?

MIKE. She said a few days was all right.

OLIVER. Where yer from?

MIKE. Prison.

OLIVER. Knew it. What for?

MIKE. Murder.

OLIVER. 'Ave t' lock our doors at night. So what's the business?

MIKE. I was in nick with 'er son.

OLIVER. Ah. Well. Serves yer right for doin murder. Yer ain stoppin. I got the spare room.

MIKE. Why d'yer come 'ere?

OLIVER. I drop in. (*Shrug.*) Me lady 'eaves me out when Im obnoxious.

MIKE. Why d'e 'ang 'isself?

OLIVER. Little prick got it right for once. (*Shrug.*) All the rackets inside. Mixed up in somethin.

MIKE. Why'd'e knife yer eye?

OLIVER. Bloody 'ell! Leave it eh? (*An angry gesture – he controls it immediately.*) Party got out a' 'and. Under all the Mr Fix-it stuff 'e was crude. Couldnt 'andle knives.

MIKE. Why did 'e –

OLIVER. Forget it. 'E's out a' it – I live with it. One eye, two a' the rest? Always gets a pint. The big joker! I carry 'im round with me. One eye, yer twist yer neck t' see all the time – gives yer a slight deformity. Pretty Polly! I got a dead man's 'and on me shoulder. The longer 'e's dead, the more 'e's there. Lets 'ope 'e dont go for the neck. They'll bury me with the bastard.

MIKE. Why go an' sleep in 'is room?

OLIVER. Same difference. If they take yer leg yer spend the rest a' yer life 'oppin after it. When they take yer eye they get right inside. Talk t' 'im when Im drunk. Give us the price of a pint an I'll ask 'im why 'e done it. Not every ventriloquist 'as a dead dummy.

The front door is heard opening and closing.

OLIVER. Dont let on what we said.

ELLEN *comes in with a parcel. She wears a street coat.*

ELLEN. 'Lo. You two all right?

MIKE. Listenin t' 'is patter. 'E should do the clubs.

ELLEN *goes into the kitchen.*

OLIVER. I told yer not t' upset 'er. Bin through enough with that bastard for a son. I dont blame 'er for this. I knew 'e was crude. There was a moment in the fight when 'e went out a control – an I missed it.

Front doorbell. ELLEN *comes from the kitchen wearing a pinafore.*

ELLEN. You expectin?
OLIVER. Yer bin followed. (*Wolf whistle.*)

ELLEN *goes through the hall door. Off, the sound of the front door and voices.*

OLIVER (*calls*). Tell 'em we ain buyin.

ELLEN *comes in and shuts the door behind her.*

ELLEN. The police. Shall I say you're here? Perhaps the probation –

The door opens behind her and FRANK *comes in in uniform.*

FRANK (*to* ELLEN). He lodging here?
MIKE. What is it Frank?
FRANK (*suddenly finds it difficult to speak. Hides it*). Change of abode sir – should be notified.
MIKE. I was going round. Who told you I was 'ere?
FRANK (*looks at* OLIVER. *Turns back to* ELLEN. *Hides under formality his difficulty in speaking*). I'd advise you not to shelter him madam. He assaulted a woman last night.
MIKE. Ha! Is that what she said?
FRANK. Soon as I saw the state she was in it all fell into place. I knew where he'd be next. Some of them carry bits of their victim round in their pocket. Relics. You're the nearest he can get to reliving what he did without paying for it. There must be a forensic name for your role madam. He gets your sympathy and wallows in being cunning. (*Glances round. He has found his own voice.*) He sees your son swinging in every shadow in this room. That's what he's here for. He hanged him.
ELLEN. Is that true? . . . You've found something out?

FRANK. He put the rope up. So he's holding the smoking gun and the dead man pulled the trigger?

ELLEN. Is that all you know? Nothing new? (*No answer.*) No! What d'you want? I won't listen!

ELLEN *goes into the kitchen.*

FRANK (*calls after her*). Your son couldnt've killed himself – he was going out! (*Turns to* MIKE.) It clicked when I saw that woman. Your first day. You cant keep your hands off.

OLIVER. Hoo hoo hoo now its interesting.

FRANK *goes into the kitchen. His and* ELLEN's *voices are heard.*

ELLEN (*off*). Go away! I wont go through all this again! You know nothing!

FRANK (*off*). You should be grateful madam. I've told you the truth about your son!

MIKE. 'E's mad.

ELLEN (*off*). Leave me alone! Leave me!

FRANK (*off*). Im not leaving you with him! A public danger! (*A door slams.*) I saw that woman! I know when someone's been terrorized. Too scared to come to the door. I had to climb to a window. *She* welcomed him with open arms: he *crept* in here! – god knows what he'll do!

OLIVER. Naughty naughty.

ELLEN (*off*). Get out of my way!

FRANK (*off*). He's got nothing to lose! They'll stick him away for life because of that woman! Rape! Assault! Think what goes on in the head of a man like that!

ELLEN *comes through without her pinafore and putting on her street coat.* FRANK *follows her.*

ELLEN. Leave me alone!

FRANK. But madam –

OLIVER. Love it. Love it.

ELLEN. I'll go to your superiors!

OLIVER. Better than the boozer!

FRANK. What sort of mother are you? Would your son

invite his killer in his house? You're in more danger than he was! Why should he kill himself when –

ELLEN. Because he was afraid! He was a boy (*Sweeping glance to* OLIVER.) – someone threatened. (*Turns away buttoning up her coat.*) Find out who threatened him! Then come here! (*Silence as she finishes fastening the last buttons.* OLIVER *and* FRANK *stare at her.*) Who sent him the letter? After that they all joined in. You know what prisons are! They terrorized him. Played with him till he –. (*To* MIKE.) You didn't kill him? Tell me!

OLIVER. 'Old on, 'old on! *I* wrote a letter – thass what you mean! I didn't write a letter! 'E topped 'isself because 'e knew what 'e'd do next time 'e 'ad a blade in 'is 'and! Why should I touch 'im? 'E'd come to a rotten end without *me* for a pen pal!

MIKE. I couldnt kill 'im! 'E could kick me t' matchwood!

FRANK. Murderers have the strength of a mob. Everyone knows that.

OLIVER. Not 'avin that pinned on me. Suffered enough for that bastard.

ELLEN. You couldnt kill him! – then come and let me take you in – treat you like my – ! *But you gave him the rope!* You never explain it! Did you kill him?

MIKE. No.

FRANK. How d'you know?

MIKE. For chrissake! I told the inquest what –

FRANK. How d'you know?

MIKE. I didnt do it!

FRANK. Perhaps you forgot.

MIKE. Forgot? 'E's mad! 'Ow could yer do that an' forget! Forget yer'd –. (*He stops. Realises. He gets up and walks away.*) No . . . its not like that . . . I didnt 'urt 'im . . . I wouldnt 'arm a . . . Dont let them say I did it. Please give me some 'elp. A little 'elp. Accusing, accusing. On an on, always accusin . . . Someone speak for me. I didnt kill 'im or my daughter. We learn when we get older – we know what we've done. Dont we? Surely? Isnt there something we can know?

FRANK (*reassurance*). I've got his number.

MIKE. I cant go through it again. Im not strong now. This 'appened when they died. I was in this place. *Its 'ere*.

ELLEN. What is it? Tell me!

MIKE. Go away! You've no right 'ere! All of you! Leave me with them! They know what I am! Sheila! The boy! . . . (*He stretches his hands as if he touched them.*)

OLIVER. Bloody 'ell! The bloody limit! 'E wants us out! 'E wants this place!

ELLEN *goes out through the hall. The front door is heard.*

FRANK. I'll tell you the truth. That woman: I saw the state she's in. She's covering up. She'll come round. There'll be charges. Now this! I started it – but it was waiting to be started. I know how it would've ended if I hadnt been here. Look at her running away! When you're around they're running from the morgue! Why did you come here? With you its always that first morning – when you killed – and phoned me. The body was under your feet. You forgot. You dont know what you do. I know. I know what its like to be *killed* by you: when you gave me your flat you were chucking flowers on my hearse. Why do I talk to you? I'll put you inside for ever.

FRANK *goes out through the hall. Door heard.* OLIVER *goes to the sideboard and looks in a vase.*

OLIVER (*turns the vase upside down. Its empty*). Keeps 'er change there. You 'ad it? No you'd 'a took the vase. If yer lent us a tenner I could leave yer in peace? You're not strapped for readies. Your sort stash it away for when they come out. Robbed the taxi driver last night. (*No answer.*) That copper's mad. They dont notice cause 'a the uniform. I could blackmail you. Tell 'im what 'e wants t' 'ear. Me eyes goin t' throb. Does that when Im upset. All that shoutin. I'd swap a pint a' blood for a pint a piss flavoured with stout. Givvus, givvus. (*Sits in the armchair facing* MIKE.) God rot this place. If I go out I come back. Stuck with 'er – another nutter. No wonder people top

theirselves. It wouldnt take much, it wouldnt take much.
Cant even cry – one eye cant cope with all I feel. If I did a
muggin I'd be Jack the Ripper. After the torments I suffer
Im supposed t' 'ave sympathy for others. They take yer
eye an yer 'ave t' be a saint.

Section Four – Stairway of Ellen's Flat

*A little later. A flight of stairs and a landing where a corridor
joins.*

A door slams in an upper storey. Clattering feet. OLIVER *comes
downstairs singing short phrases to calm his anger. He comes into
view getting into his jacket.* FRANK *steps out of the passage-
way.*

OLIVER. O yeh? Waitin for 'er? (*Going on.*) Dont talk t'
nutters.
FRANK (*following him for a few paces. Functionally*). Want
to earn?
OLIVER (*stops*). Shop 'im? 'Ow much?
FRANK. I cant prove he strung up the lad. I'll get him but
it'll be late. If he gave you a hammering I'd get him –
OLIVER. Give us a tenner. We'll 'ave a natter sometime. Do
business. In a 'urry now.
FRANK. – and you apply to the criminal injuries board.
Second time victim. You'd clean them out.
OLIVER. No one give me for the eye.
FRANK. No board then.
OLIVER. You rough me up – I point the finger at 'im – an I
get paid?
FRANK. We use her flat. Call me when they're out – I'll
give you a number. Bit of damage. Few bruises. Your
word against his. His record? Open and shut.
OLIVER. 'Ow much?
FRANK. Thousands.
OLIVER. Sound nice people. What do I lose? Its on. Lend
us a tenner an I'll pay yer back when I get me money.

FRANK. D'you want the number or not? Memorise it. Nothing written down.

Section Five – Ellen's Living Room/The Grey Room 'Training'

A few days later. Evening. Electric light. OLIVER in sweat shirt, slacks and runners. He picks up the phone and his face concentrates as he recalls the number and dials.

Half an hour later. OLIVER leads FRANK into the room. FRANK is in police uniform.

FRANK. How long?
OLIVER. 'Bout an 'our. Probation's give 'im a late appointment.

FRANK *takes off his jacket.*

FRANK. Uniform. Mustn't mark. (*He takes off his shirt and trousers.*)
OLIVER. . . . Dont wan' it too rough.
FRANK. Got to be genuine. No pay otherwise. More you take the more you get.
OLIVER. I know, I know. I know all that. They always pay? Government dont run out a money? Dont trust that lot.

FRANK *picks up the TV set and gives it to* OLIVER.

FRANK. Break it. (OLIVER *looks at him.*) Go on. Get the adrenalin pumpin. Charges the atmosphere. Dont feel it then. Like takin the medicine before you're hurt. Fact. I could cut off your dick and you wouldnt know till you kissed the girlfriend goodnight. (OLIVER *hesitates.*) Break a few things.

OLIVER *breaks the TV. He giggles.* FRANK *hands him some glasses from the sideboard.*

FRANK. Break them.

OLIVER *breaks the glasses.*

FRANK. You've got it. Bright lad!

FRANK *gives* OLIVER *a chair.*

OLIVER. An that?

FRANK. Smash it. They'll pay. Its your money. Smash it.
Smash it. Smash it.

FRANK *hits* OLIVER *in the face.*

OLIVER. O yer bastard!

OLIVER *smashes the chair.* FRANK *takes a looking glass
from the sideboard and gives it to* OLIVER.

FRANK. Smash it.

OLIVER. Yeh. But not so rough. That 'urt.

FRANK. You're a time waster – plonker! (*Hits* OLIVER *in
the face.*) Smash it. You're not smashing enough. That's
why it hurt. Your fault!

OLIVER *smashes the looking glass.* FRANK *kicks him.*

FRANK. That 'urt?

OLIVER. Ow bastard! (OLIVER *kicks* FRANK.) That 'urt
– like *that!*

FRANK. . . . We're getting nasty. Down to the little worm.

FRANK *punches* OLIVER.

OLIVER. Bastard.

FRANK *gives* OLIVER *china ornaments.*

FRANK. Smash it! Smash it! Smash it! Or I'll break your
bloody neck!

OLIVER (*Shying china at the walls*). Bastards! Bastards!
Why did I get in t' this? Bastards! Smash it!

FRANK *attacks* OLIVER *viciously.* OLIVER *retaliates on
the furniture.*

OLIVER (*smashing*). Bastard! Bastard! Bastard! The bastard's 'ittin me! The bastards! I'll kill the bloody lot! O 'er
poor stuff – she paid for that – that was a bit a' – 'ad it for
years –. (*Stops. Cries.*) Enough. 'S enough.

FRANK. This? Its junk! Junk! It should be smashed!

OLIVER. We done enough.

FRANK. You wimp! Your money! They owe you for the eye!

The grey room.

The action is continuous. FRANK *and* OLIVER *are in a large grey space with plain walls and a ceiling. The doors are dark blanks. The debris and furniture are the same as in the first room, and the same pictures hang on the walls.*

OLIVER. The bastards! The bloody bastards took my eye! Where are they? Pay what yer owe me! Smash it! Smash it! Smash it!

FRANK *grabs* OLIVER's *collar and shakes and mauls him.*

FRANK. Come 'ere yer little bastard! Yer couldnt shake 'ands with a fractured wrist! (*Hits* OLIVER *in the back of the neck.*)

OLIVER (*screams with shock.*) You bastard! (*He hits* FRANK.)

FRANK. You little dog. You dangerous little tyke. That'll cost. You'll pay for that. Hit me you bastard? Im the law! (*He uses his fist as a hammer to beat* OLIVER *down.*) Came here. On a public service. (*Hammering.*) Line your pockets. Put that bastard away. (*Kicks* OLIVER.) And you hit me! (*Walks away from* OLIVER, *turns and faces him.*) Gratitude? (*He takes a running kick at* OLIVER.) Say sorry sir you nasty bit of snot!

OLIVER (*dodging*). I'll murder yer! I'll bloody kill yer! When I get me money! I'll bloody run yer down! I'll run yer under the bloody road!

FRANK. Run me down? Yer couldnt run yer finger up yer nose t' pick it! (*Gestures round.*) Bomb it!

OLIVER *goes wild and smashes up the place.* FRANK *follows him round encouraging him with hits and kicks.*

OLIVER. Bomb it! Bomb it! Bomb it!

FRANK. Bomb it! Bomb it! All this! All yours! Your

kingdom! Bomb it! You little shit! King shit – are we?
Come 'ere!

FRANK *puts both hands on top of* OLIVER's *head and
forces him down to a standing crouch.* OLIVER *protects his
head, sides and crutch with his hands and arms.* FRANK
moves round him kicking and punching him.

FRANK. You bastard! Threaten me! The best pal you got! I
give you money money money money money money!

OLIVER (*through clenched teeth, as if repeating his prayers
weakly*). Money . . . money . . . money . . .

FRANK. The face! The face! The face! Give me the face! I
want the face!

OLIVER *stands in the same crouch. Slowly he raises his face
– eyes and mouth screwed tight.* FRANK *takes a breath and
hits his face. Repeatedly.*

OLIVER. O dear. O please. O god no please. Dont. Sir.
Dont.

FRANK. Love it! Love it! Scum! Its good for you you snot!
Its money!

OLIVER (*crying*). No more . . . I'll make the bastards
pay . . .

OLIVER *turns to hobble away.* FRANK *trips him.*
OLIVER *falls.*

FRANK. Get up! Get up!

OLIVER *stands and heaves over a table.*

OLIVER. Pay! Pay! Pay! Pay!

OLIVER *picks up an empty broken frame and clutches it to
himself for comfort.* FRANK *hits him with a chair.* OLIVER
sprawls into the debris and lies still.

FRANK. Get up. (*Kicks* OLIVER.) The man's berserk.
Killer. Attacks women. What sort of man's that? (*Walks
round surveying the mess.*) Yes . . . Yes . . . Not bad . . .
Looks good . . . A mess . . . His footprints everywhere.
(*He chucks a broken cup at* OLIVER.) Look! My god – no

wonder we need prisons: thugs like you . . . (*Smashes a glass.*) Bit of law and order. That'll do. Phew. You lucky man. They'll ram it down your throat. Piss the milk of human kindness.

OLIVER (*flat*). I cant see.

FRANK. Soon's he's in the door. Dial 999. Not before.

OLIVER *is still sprawled in the debris.*

OLIVER. I cant see.

FRANK. Tell them what I said. Dont embellish. The woman'll back you up. Goes berserk, out of the blue. Lost my cap. (*Searches.*) In this junk. If that's marked I'll thump you for real! . . . I could do with some water.

OLIVER. I cant see.

FRANK (*looks at him*). Get the blood off your –. (*He goes to OLIVER and gets down beside him.*) Ugh. Wipe your mug. (*Searches for a rag. Finds his cap. Brushes it.*) Dirt. (*Puts it on.*) Wipe your –. (*Finds a rag.*) God's sake yer look like a dead rat in a drain.

OLIVER. I cant see.

FRANK (*giving OLIVER the rag*). Get a grip of yourself! Mind my jacket you oaf! (*Pushing the rag into OLIVER's hand.*) For chrissake! – catch hold of this. What're you going to tell them? Everything depends on that!

The rag falls from OLIVER's hand. His hand feels round to find where he is. He doesnt hear FRANK. His voice does not change – flat, rather like a child's.

OLIVER. I cant see.

FRANK. No – cause you're running in muck! (*He tries to force the rag into OLIVER's hand.*) Wipe yourself. Im not paddling in your gore. Blood's too dodgy these days.

OLIVER. I cant see.

FRANK. There must be some concussion. (*He kneels by OLIVER.*) You knocked your head and –. Shake your head – clear it. (*He grabs OLIVER's head and shakes it. Then he cuffs it.*) Look. (*He waves his finger in front of OLIVER's face.*) My finger. (*To himself.*) O god he's . . .

(*Clenches his fists and bangs the heels of his palms together. Triumph.*) He's lost an eye . . . The other eye! I've got him! Fixed him! He'll go down for – yipppeeee! (*Pity for OLIVER.*) And. Wipe it. Wipe it. It may not be. Wipe. You'll see. I promise – your pal – you'll – and spend the money.

OLIVER (*not hearing FRANK*). I cant see.

FRANK (*low, gleeful*). He cant see! He cant see! He –. Tell me its true! (*Shock.*) O god my uniform . . . (*Stands. Moves away taking off his jacket. Puts it down. Dances a few steps.*) He cant see! (*Goal-scorer's triumph: bends back his head, bends his knees and elbows and shakes his clenched fists.*) I did it! I scored! (*Pity. Goes to OLIVER.*) O no no no no its nothing – only a little – you poor – poor – it'll pass – they'll make it go.

OLIVER. I cant see.

FRANK. I didnt want this. I only needed a little –. Not necessary for my –. You know I didnt want it. (*Tries to control himself.*) The time. Late. (*To OLIVER.*) I didnt do it. You threw yourself about and –. Did it to yourself. We nailed him the main thing is we . . . (*Still trying to be calm.*) So you suffer. He's mad. They all suffer if he's not put away. What is the story? Tell me.

OLIVER. I cant see.

OLIVER *crawls round the floor in a circle trying to reach the door.* FRANK *walks round in the opposite direction.*

FRANK. Shut in. Shut in. This prison. With that. O god what shall I do? Could I –? He broke the telly and got into a – no control. Useless. Useless. I work with trash. The job's impossible.

OLIVER *reaches the wall and tries to climb it.*

FRANK. O god he's going for a doctor! Now I've got to be his nurse! (*He goes to OLIVER.*) All right. All right. Im here. (*He examines OLIVER's face.*) Im trained. Medical work. Keep still. (*Dabs OLIVER's eye with the rag.*) How can I help you if –? Waste time getting to a doctor.

Attention now. (*Stares at the wounded eye.*) O god its beautiful . . . (*Gently touches the wound.*) How kind. My life. Its beautiful . . . (*He hangs his head in awe.*) They'll take twenty year from him for this . . .

ELLEN'*s living room.*

The action is continuous. OLIVER *crawls away along the bottom of the wall. From time to time he tries to climb it and edge along – he falls.* FRANK *watches him crawl – then follows him, squatting and moving forward on his haunches, leaning over him, sometimes rising when he rises, sometimes looking up at him.*

FRANK. You must hear this. Your eye's bad. I think. I know. You're blind. Perhaps. *You're blind. Face it* – get it over. Stick to the story. Your only chance. You need money now – you know that more than I do. You're lucky. The story's gone up in price. Its worth hundreds of thousands now. Im sorry – people like him – there's no defence against the – that's the world. (*He stands and combs his hair.*) Now listen. (Am I talking to myself?) My superiors'll never own up to this. The force'll stick behind me. They'll hound you till you wish you had another eye to give them. You tell the truth an' you get nothing. Even if they believe you. You entered a criminal conspiracy with me: nothing! Tell the story. Its your big chance. You're rich.

OLIVER. I cant see.

FRANK (*grips* OLIVER). What is the story? (*He lets* OLIVER *go. Tired.*) You're on your own. I've got to go. Do what you like: you attacked me – I hit you in self defence.

FRANK *picks up his jacket, goes to the middle of the room and crouches on his haunches to think.*

FRANK. So still. I havent got the strength to walk downstairs: and I've got to put up all the bluff. Some good'll come of it. (*Suddenly becomes very weary.*) Some day people'll be good – no violence then. I try. I take the risk. It always ends in mess. One house I kicked a door down, when we brought the villain out the rats were feeding on the splinters. Its him. He killed her. It comes from him. Sometimes Im frightened of myself. I dont know where its going. (*Fingers the dust.*) Dee-dum. Dee-dum. (*He looks calmly at* OLIVER.) Can I trust him? That's why you chose him. Little crooks take the money.

The sound of the front door.

FRANK. O god.

FRANK *gets up and goes into the kitchen.*

MIKE *comes in holding his jacket in his hand. He stops.*

OLIVER *sits on the ground like a doll with his back to the wall and his legs stretched out before him. The bloody rag is on his knee. His hands stray feebly over the floor and walls. He has not heard* MIKE.

OLIVER. I cant see.

MIKE *takes a few steps towards him, half crouches and holds out a hand. A sound behind him: steps on broken glass. He turns.*

FRANK *is coming out of the kitchen towards* MIKE. *He wears his cap and uniform and has tied Ellen's pinafore over it.* MIKE *stands as he reaches him. He viciously punches* MIKE *twice in the face, takes the jacket from his hand, rips open a pocket, tears a lapel and throws the jacket onto* OLIVER. *He stares at* MIKE *a moment and then speaks – at the normal speed, but he is so exhausted that no sound comes out of his mouth.*

FRANK (*silent*). Im tired.

He backs, takes off the pinafore, drops it and – still calm – goes out to the hall. The sound of the front door.

Section Six – Hospital Ward

Day, natural light. A small single-bed room in an NHS hospital. A locker and a visitors chair beside the bed. The bed is made up. OLIVER sits next to it in an adult version of a child's high chair; it has a table top that swings across as a gate to hold the sitter. On it, an invalid's plastic mug with a spout. OLIVER wears yellow pyjama trousers and a printed sweat shirt. His head is gauzed unevenly so that parts of it show through.

MIKE sits on the visitors chair. ELLEN sits on the edge of the bed. They wear street clothes.

MIKE (*to* OLIVER *trying to see if he remembers*). Frank? (*No answer.*) Was it? (*No answer.*) Criminal injuries pay-out? They might not. I'll tell the truth. What use is money now yer cant see? Let Elly look after yer. Yer need 'er.

No answer.

ELLEN. Olly.

No answer: OLIVER *doesn't listen to them.* ELLEN *leans forward in despair.* MIKE *puts his hand on her to comfort her.*

OLIVER (*runs his finger round the edge of the table top*). Thass the map a' my world from now on.

Section Seven – Ellen's Bedroom

Night. ELLEN *and* MIKE *in the large single bed. Naked, still.*

MIKE. The law'll speak t' 'im t'morra. 'E'll take the money. Piss it down the drain. In that state yer cant see anyway. When its gone he'll fall down on your doorstep – you send 'im away?

ELLEN. 'E cant sit in the dark year after year knowin 'e put you back inside . . . The blind cant lie . . .

MIKE. I've got some of the answers now. Frank murdered my daughter an' your son. 'E wasnt there when it 'appened – didnt 'ave t' be. 'E did it – just as 'e blinded

Olly. For the same reason. 'Ow can I make anyone understand that? See the connections. They cant. That's why we go on sufferin. Olly's prison. 'E'll never get out. We're all in it till we understand.

Stage Version

The play was written for TV. A few changes are necessary for the stage. Most of these are in Part Two. The Association Area takes up most of the stage. The visiting rooms are to one side, Mike's cell to the other. The cupboard is upstage. It has two doors, one to the front and one to the rear.

The hallways and stairs in Parts One and Three should be cut.

In Part One it is possible (but not necessary) to cut the day that passes between Sections Two and Three. Section Three could begin with Mike at the door opening it to Frank. Later in the section 'day' would have to be changed to 'night' in Frank's lines 'Have you sat there all day – ' and 'No you wouldnt sit there all day if you'd disturbed a . . .'. At the end of Section Two Mike's line 'This evening' would have to be changed to 'Soon as you can'.

It might seem that difficulties are created for the stage by the destruction in Part Three, Section Five, and the shortness of the following two Sections. The difficulties may be turned to advantage. The destruction is not an indulgence in chaotic violence. It is a lesson in destructiveness, taught by Authority. Authority carefully chooses the objects to be broken. Its actions have precise aims. It trains its victim efficiently. It is not till the end that it becomes its own victim. I saw a rehearsal in which the fight was staged as a 'TV punch up'. It was disastrous. It showed that Authority owned even the violence on TV and made it a commercial product. It did not show the social cause and psychological cost of violence. There was no 'Theatre Event' (TE) of the sort I have described in the Commentary to my *War Plays*.

Sections Six and Seven should be staged 'ruthlessly' in the chaos of the living room. Anything needed to create the different venues should be done and shown openly. There should be no attempt to create an illusion of naturalism. Naturalism is created from fictions, from the illusion of reality. Theatre must show the reality of this illusion. When it does this it changes reality – the fictions by which we live. Fiction, illusion, false pretences – these are the enemies of art.

PART ONE

Section Two – Living-Room

Morning. Daylight comes through the drawn curtains. SHEILA lies face down on the table with the cup beside her. MIKE sleeps slumped in the armchair. A doorbell. He does not react. A few moments pass and he opens his eyes and concentrates, trying to recall if he has heard a sound. The doorbell again. He gets up, notices the curtains are drawn and opens them. He goes downstage right to the door that leads onto the outside stairs. He opens it. VERA stands there. She is about thirty and wears slippers and indoor clothes.

VERA. Rang four times. Standing there. Your curtains are drawn.

MIKE. What time is it.

VERA. You'll be asking me what day it is next. Thought you were working this weekend. I cant stop. Came to see Sheila. (*Passes by him into the room.*) She up?

MIKE (*remembers. He spins round on the spot to stare after VERA*). No no she's not – you cant –

As VERA walks into the room she sees SHEILA slumped as before on the table.

VERA. She drunk? She's not starting all that? Sheila . . .!

(*No other changes in the scene.*)

Section Three – Living-Room
'The Hand on the Telephone'

That evening. Darkish. Doorbell. Immediately MIKE stands, goes downstage right to the door and opens it. FRANK is there.

FRANK. Well – what was so urgent?

(*No other changes in the section.*)

PART TWO

Section One – Visiting Room in a Closed Prison

A table with two chairs. VERA and MIKE sit facing each other. There is a barrier between them across the table. Two Prison Officers – one on a high stool – watch upstage.

(No other changes in the section.)

Section Two – Association Area

Day. A bleak space. Tables, chairs, a few games. The Association Area is empty except for MIKE and BARRY sitting at adjoining tables. MIKE is turned away with a vacant expression. SMILER comes in. He seems under twenty and is blond, good-looking and at home in the world. He crosses the Association Area with a mug of tea.

Later, when MIKE gets up and slowly walks away, he goes to his cell and lies on his bed.

(No other changes in the section.)

Section Three – Mike's Cell

MIKE *is lying on one of the two beds.* SMILER *passes, glances in at* MIKE *and goes on. After a few seconds he comes back. He leans on the end of* BARRY's *bed and watches* MIKE. BARRY *is still bowed over his cigarette in the Association Area.*

SMILER. They keep that face in a bin an 'and it round. Year four. Yer look like snow thass bin pissed on just after they made the thaw illegal. (*Yells.*) Three days! Out! Yer're goin' t' miss me!

PRISONER 3 (*off. Friendly aggression*). Yer'll git four bloody years in 'ospital!

SMILER (*to* MIKE). Come t' say cheerio.

MIKE. Monday . . .

SMILER. Three days. If I last. Wont be time for cheerios then. (*He sits on* BARRY's *bed.*) 'Ave t' console the mob. What yer in for: frighten ol' ladies with that mug? If yer laughed yer'd go t' the medic with a dangerous symptom.

MIKE *makes a friendly, tired gesture with his hand.*

SMILER. Ain so bad: four years then its down all the way. (*Hand gesture.*) The sunny side. I'll keep yer company for a bit. That all right? (*No answer.*) Dump eh? Architect put the rat 'oles in when they built it. That ol' crap 'eap get on yer nerves? If I let 'im 'e'd smoke the 'ole camel. Way beyond 'is means. I mix it with 'im so 'e keeps out a' real bother. Even a wimp like 'im can go the distance with the champ if its shadow boxin. Puts a bit a' shape in 'is life. 'E ain grateful. (*Slight pause.*) Thass it then. (*Gestures to* MIKE *to be silent. Raises his voice slightly.*) Im goin' t' chuck all me ciggies in the air and let the lads scramble – freebies!

BARRY *patters into the cell.*

SMILER. Ain it marvellous! 'E'd 'ear a fart if a brass band was playin in a thunderstorm. (*To* BARRY.) You're so bent yer arse knows more words than yer gob.

SMILER *goes.* BARRY *mutters after him.*

BARRY. Know a few words for you.

BARRY *sits on the edge of his bed with the cigarette butt in his hand. He opens his locker and takes a pin from the shelf. He sticks the pin into the end of the butt.*

The little sod'll be back. Read 'is palm even if 'e was born with no arms. Give 'im a week. Six months at the most. You dead? Make the most of it. The chaplain says they come round an wake yer up. Dont suppose Smiler drop yer any ciggies? Might'a lashed out cause'a Monday. If 'e slashed an Jesus walked on the puddle 'e'd charge 'im for a

ticket. Know where . . . (*He lights the stub and inhales.*)
. . . 'is stash is. Dont finger it. Do it all verbal. Not mixin
it with 'im an 'is mates – even if 'is ciggies was a mile long.
Know what 'e's in for? 'E don't mind 'oo knows. Tell
anyone for a packet a' twenty. No, tell *that* for nothin –
only thing 'e dont charge for. (*He removes a shred of tobacco
from his lip and examines it on the end of his finger.*) Carved
'is mate in a bar. Mate, mind – not an outsider. Cut 'is eye
out. Not normal, like slashin a cheek. Made a proper job,
they say. Methodical. Talent for it. Would'a bin a surgeon
if 'e'd come from a proper family. Poor ol' national 'ealth.
(*He slides the shred of tobacco onto the smouldering butt.
Inhales.*) Went for the other eye. Ambitious. Mates pulled
'im off. Bloke saw 'is own eye in the broken glass. 'Ad t' go
somewhere. New meanin t' gazin in t' the crystal ball:
Smiler's little joke when 'e tells it. Comes up every time.
Know 'im from the cradle t' the gallows, as they used t'
say. (*Small wince as he burns his lip.*) Wass 'e put in 'is fags?
Fluff off a gorilla's groin. Think they're number one. The
ocean couldnt dilute the piss they talk. (*Calls.*) Smiler! –
See 'em in the visitors room. Their mothers and tarts.
White faces. Starin great eyes. Like the eyes on those tree
rats – or monkeys is it? – yer see on telly. (*Calls.*) Smiler!
(– Watch me put 'im through 'is paces.) In the visitors
room. Then they give birth t' their kids. An yer see it in
the kids. Even the little toddlers. Same little murderers'
faces. Animals're descended from 'uman bein's. (*Calls.*)
Oi! – You watch. Looks down on me cause a me 'abit.
That ash's got more life in it than their kids.

BARRY *cleans the pin.* SMILER *comes in.*

SMILER. Three days! Three! Three! Three! (*He picks up a
pillow and beats* BARRY *with it.*) Dont oi me yer git! Oi!
Oi! Oi!
BARRY. Lay off yer bleedin nutter! Yer lost me pin!
SMILER. 'Oo you oi-in'? (*Chucks the pillow down.*) Im 'ere!
BARRY. Tell us what yer'll do on Monday Smiler.
SMILER. When they say on the news there's bin an earth

tremor thass me on the job. (BARRY *finds his pin.*) One day yer'll bend that pin an 'ave a twin.

BARRY *puts the pin on the shelf of his locker and shuts the door.*

BARRY. Yer'll be down the boozer too pissed t' get the wrinkles out.

SMILER. Mine dont 'ave wrinkles grandad. Thass where I notch up the virgins. Wass it worth? All the details before I sell it t' the press?

BARRY. Tell us Smiler. You're a lad. Slip it in eh?

SMILER. Yer lecherous ol' lag! (*Yells.*) Three days! (*To* BARRY.) Forty ciggies on account?

PRISONER 1 (*off*). Put a sock in it Smiler!

PRISONER 2 (*off*). Yer sayin yer prayers?

PRISONER 1 (*off*). Pullin me plonker! Show some respect for the workin man!

SMILER (*to* BARRY). Get 'ard on it t'night? Yer couldnt get 'ard if they give yer an iron spike an cement injections. No Im not tellin you. Ain wasted time in 'ere – I learnt. Not the garbage they feed yer. I watched the lot that put us 'ere – thass where I learnt. They're the crooks – an they get away with it. They cant fail. Its their set-up – all that out there: the rich man's racket. From now on its number one. I give that poxy shower enough a' my life. Aint comin back next time. (*Yells.*) Three days! (*Off, groans. He yells.*) Out! Screwin boozin cars Costa Brava lolly!

PRISONER 2 (*off. Friendly aggression*). Thank chriss! Then we'll get a bit a' shut-eye!

BARRY. You're a lad Smiler. Slip it in eh? Tell us.

SMILER (*suddenly still*). I cant. I told yer. Screwin boozin cars trip-t'-the-sea lolly: 's foreign language in 'ere. Yer cant understand nothin in 'ere. I only know what it means cause the door's openin for out. If I tried t' tell yer its like writin on a sheet a' paper an' the words come out on the other side: all you see's blank, 's out there where it means.

BARRY. Six months. You'll be back.

SMILER (*very still*). Yer see? Yer cant understand. Givvus

givvus givvus: its freedom innit? (*Jumps up and yells.*)
What sod said put a sock in it?

SMILER *runs out. Off, prisoners' yells and shouts.* 'Shuttit
nutter!'

Section Four – Association Area – Cupboard – Mike's Cell

Night. BARRY *sleeps in his bed.* MIKE *goes to the cupboard in
the Association Area. He opens the door and goes in. The second
door at the back of the cupboard is open. He shuts it. Inside the
cupboard along one side near the top there is a shelf backed by a
wooden plank. Pipes on the walls and ceiling. A few mops,
squeegees and buckets with mop-grills in the top. Two domestic
chairs, one reversed with its seat on the seat of the other.*

MIKE *takes a rope hidden in the corner. He lifts down the top
chair and stands it under a pipe that crosses the ceiling. He starts
to tie the rope-end into a noose. He is weak and sits on the chair to
finish it. He climbs onto the chair. From a trousers side-pocket he
takes a small envelope – blue, crinkled, with worn edges. He
props it against the plank behind the shelf.*

*He passes the end of the rope over the pipe on the ceiling and knots
it. For a moment he stands in silence. His hand strays to his side
in the gesture of a child that wants to pee. He steps down from the
chair – and doing this moves it so that it is no longer directly under
the noose.*

MIKE *leaves the cupboard. He closes the door behind him. He
crosses the Association Area and goes to his cell. He picks up the
night bucket. He carefully urinates against the side, making no
sound.*

PRISON OFFICER 1 *comes into the Association Area. He is
bent and grey. He carries a large stack of files before him in both
hands. He drops a sheet from one of the files but does not notice.
He goes out.*

MIKE *goes back to the Association Area. He sees the sheet of paper on the ground. He stops. He stares at it dully. He steps over it. He goes to the cupboard. Calmly he opens the door.*

SMILER *is hanging in the noose. The door on the far side of the cupboard is wide open. A chair lies on its side under the body. The other chair is where* MIKE *had left it.* MIKE *runs into the cupboard. He tries to support the body and loosen the noose. He cant. The body swings round, twisting away from him as if its fighting him.* MIKE *whimpers and tries to support it and hook the chair towards him with his foot but his foot pushes it further away. He lets the body swing, picks up the chair, stands it by the body and climbs onto it. He tugs the body toward him. The legs flop against the chair – it almost topples. He hitches the weight of the body off the rope and loosens it. He drags it over the face, squashing and grazing the nose and cheeks and yanking open the mouth. He stands on the chair holding the body and breathes into its mouth. He climbs down. The chair lurches from under him, crashes into the wall and bounces away. He stumbles to the ground with the body and falls on top of it. He shakes it.*

MIKE. Smiler. Smiler. No. No. (*Stands, lost, blank.*) I – where is the –? What 'ave –? (*Looks down at the body. Slowly he kneels by the body, hits the chest, breathes into the mouth.*) Please.

MIKE *stands. Looks round, sees the chair, picks it up, puts it under the noose and starts to climb onto it: one leg tangles with the body, the foot of the leg pressed into its hand.*

MIKE. No! No! Let go! Give me the chair! I will! I will!

MIKE *savagely kicks the body away – the chair is free. He climbs onto it and reaches for the noose. It is much larger than it was – stretched when it was pulled from the head.* MIKE *holds the bottom of the noose with both hands and pulls it open so that it forms a perfect equilateral triangle. He holds the bottom straight and pulls down to keep the triangle rigid. He puts his head into it. He feels with his foot to kick the chair away.*

MIKE's *hands grip the bottom of the triangle as if it were a rail. Pause. Suddenly his face cracks – it seems to burst into pieces – and water pours from his eyes and the cracks as if his face were breaking up and washing away in a flood. Dribble spills from his mouth. He makes a sound. Slowly he lets go of the rope, creeps down from the chair, huddles against a wall and cries.*

MIKE *runs out of the cupboard into the Association Area.*

MIKE. 'Elp! 'Elp! 'Elp! You bastards! 'E's dyin!

MIKE *runs back into the cupboard, kneels by the body and breathes into its mouth.*

PRISON OFFICER 1 *and* PRISON OFFICER 2 *run into the Association Area.*

MIKE. 'E pulled the chair when I stood on the –
PRISON OFFICER 1. Out!
MIKE. 'E's alive!
PRISON OFFICER 2. Out! Out! Out!

PRISON OFFICER 2 *pulls* MIKE *from the body and throws him from the cupboard. An alarm siren starts.* PRISON OFFICER 1 *kneels by the body and gives expert resuscitation treatment.* MIKE *gets to his feet.* PRISON OFFICER 3 *comes in, goes to the cupboard and looks in. He says nothing. Prisoners are heard shouting.*

PRISONER 2 (*off*). Whass up?
PRISONER 3 (*off*). 'Oo they got?
PRISONERS (*off*). Bastards! Bastards! 'Oo is it? What they up to? Dont want witnesses!

The Prisoners kick and hammer the cell doors. Shouts. PRISON OFFICER 1 *interrupts his resuscitation drill for a moment.*

PRISON OFFICER 1 (*to* PRISON OFFICER 3, *calmly*). Kill that bloody racket. Ain wakin 'im up an its givin me an earache.

MIKE *goes to his cell. He half-sits, half-crouches on his bed with his face to the wall and gasps as if he had just run round the world.* BARRY *sits upright and motionless on his bed watching him. MIKE's hand slides along the bed, he levers himself up and to the side and slowly, still crying – without fuss, like a mechanical toy – crawls off the bed, creeps under it and goes out of sight.*

BARRY does not move, he stares at the bed – then he stands and creeps on tiptoe to the Association Area.

PRISON OFFICER 3 (*yells*). Shurrup! 'Eads down! Bloody shut-eye!

PRISONER 3 (*off*). Dont bloody shush me!

PRISONER 2 (*off*). 'Oo they got?

PRISON OFFICER 3 (*yells*). Shut it or they'll be trouble!

PRISONER 2 (*off*). 'E said dyin!

PRISONER 1 (*off*). 'S'a rope!

PRISONER 3 (*off*). Rope!

PRISONER 2. Another one!

The prisoners shout and bang in unison.

PRISONERS (*off*). Rope! Rope! Rope! Rope! Rope!

PRISON OFFICER 3 (*yells*). No rope!

PRISONER 2 (*off*). Massacre!

PRISON OFFICER 2 (*yells*). 'S'n'accident!

PRISONER 1 (*off*). Listen! Listen! Shurrup!

PRISONERS (*off*). Shurrup! Listen! Rope! Murder! Bastards!

PRISONER 1 (*off*). Shut it! Listen what's goin on! That's what they dont want! Listen!

PRISONERS (*off*). Rope! Listen! Listen!

The Prisoners are silent. The alarm siren stops. PRISON OFFICER 1 works at resuscitation. PRISON OFFICER 2 and PRISON OFFICER 3 stoop over the body. In the silence MIKE is heard under the bed. He sobs in a brief downward scale.

MIKE (*unseen*). Uh – uh – uh – uh – uh.

PRISONER 3 (*off*). Rope!

PRISONER 2 (*off*). Shut it! Listen! I'll bloody rope *you*!

A few Prisoners shout 'Rope' and others shout 'Shut it!'. A

*communal hiss as the Prisoners call for silence. Silence.
BARRY is peering into the cupboard. PRISON OFFICER 1
looks up and sees him.*

PRISON OFFICER 1 (*half-weary*). 'Op it scrag!

PRISON OFFICER 3 *frog-marches* BARRY *to his cell.*
PRISON OFFICER 1 *stops the resuscitation drill.*

PRISON OFFICER 2. 'Ad t' choose the end a' shift!

PRISON OFFICER 1. 'E's gone t' the great prison in the
sky.

PRISON OFFICER 2 *sees the envelope on the shelf. He
takes it down.*

PRISON OFFICER 2. Remembered t' post early for Chrissmass. Shall I . . .?

PRISON OFFICER 1. 'Is thank you letter. (*He takes the
letter and opens it.*)

PRISONER 4 (*off*). Whass 'appening?

PRISONER 3 (*off*). Rope!

PRISON OFFICER 1. Might've left a forwardin address
. . . (*He takes a note from the envelope and sees the signature.*)
No 'e aint.

Section Five – Mike's Cell

The next day. BARRY *and* MIKE *alone.* BARRY *sits on his
bed. He has an open suitcase on it in front of him. In the suitcase,
assorted packets of about eight hundred cigarettes. A few more
packets on the bed by the case.*

BARRY (*gazing at the packets*). Could' a left 'im me pin in me
will. (*Looks up at* MIKE.) Know where 'e 'kep 'em 'id?
That cupboard. Be'ind the board on the shelf. Not some
little bog 'ole. Move arf the wall t' get at 'em. Smart.

MIKE *takes no notice of* BARRY. *He stands head bowed in
thought. Suddenly* BARRY *jerks a blanket over the case and*

the loose packets. A few seconds later PRISON OFFICER 2 *comes in.*

PRISON OFFICER 2 (*to* MIKE). Visitor.

Section Six – Probation Office – Association Area – Mike's Cell
'Four Lumps of Sugar'

A table and two chairs. ELLEN *enters with two mugs of coffee and four lumps of sugar. She puts the mugs on the table and the four lumps of sugar by the cups. She stands and waits.* PRISON OFFICER 2 *brings* MIKE *in.* MIKE *sits at the table.* PRISON OFFICER *waits outside.*

(*No other changes till the end.*)

ELLEN *reads the note as he holds it in his hand.*

MIKE. A copy. Wouldn't give me the original. Thass the property a' the court.

ELLEN *goes without looking at* MIKE *or speaking to him.* PRISON OFFICER 3 *comes in.*

PRISON OFFICER 3. Take that with yer.

MIKE *stands. He picks up the two coffee mugs. He goes towards his cell.* PRISON OFFICER *follows him.* MIKE *stops. He stares dully at the two coffee mugs.*

PRISON OFFICER 3. Move. Paralytic twat. (*No response.*) Move!

MIKE *goes into his cell. He puts the two coffee cups on top of the locker. He lies on his bed facing away from them.* BARRY *is not there.* PRISON OFFICER 3 *goes out.*

Section Seven

Delete.

Section Eight – Visiting Room in an Open Prison

*Day. A table with two chairs. PRISON OFFICER 5 sits
upstage and reads a newspaper. From time to time, the sounds of
visiting children and their mothers.*

*VERA sits at the table. She wears a brown coat and a baggy
beret of loosely knitted pale string. MIKE stands at the table and
looks towards the door.*

VERA. Arent you excited?

MIKE. Yer said Frank was comin.

VERA. Outside, bein tactful. Sit down.

MIKE. Whass 'e want?

VERA. Didnt bring anything. Only extra t' carry out. Yer
dont want to leave anything behind. He hasnt said.

MIKE sits.

VERA. Hardly seen him since he sold me your flat. Found
him on the front door in his uniform. I knew he joined the
police when he moved. I thought: panic – he wants the flat
back! The thoughts go through your head! The flat's
mine. He cant touch it. Payments up to date. He wanted
me to ask you to send him a visiting order. Suppose he
wouldnt write to you direct in case you said no. They train
the police in social work now. He'll offer to stand by you,
say he doesnt hold a grudge. Ask me, he owes *you*: you
gave him the flat. He certainly didnt think of that when he
sold it to me!

MOTHER (*off*). Lucy come an kiss da-da bub-bye. Got to
catch our train.

VERA. Cant wait to see your face when you see the flat. All
new – even the –! No you'll see it for yourself! I had to
struggle. You're worth it. (*She is going to pat his hand but
doesnt.*) This isnt the place for emotions. Frank'll know
what to do if you get into trouble.

MIKE. I wont get into trouble.

VERA. We wont let you. As long as you dont get upset – and
dont try to do everything yourself. Its all changed. Ten

years is what ten lifetimes used to be. A day or two's rest, then we'll look for a job. Wont rush it. Two to keep, and the mortgage. We wont have a kid, you dont want to be bothered with that again. You wont believe the prices. Frank brought me in the car. I'd love to know what he's after. Wouldnt let me help toward the petrol. I'll pop out and send him in. Make a note of everything he says. He might drop little hints you dont understand. All right?

VERA *stands and goes towards the door.* MIKE *watches her. At the door she turns to mouth, emphasizing the words with stabs of her index finger: 'Dont worry – it'll be all right – I'll be back soon'.* MIKE *stares at the door after she has gone.*

MOTHER (*off*). Lucy! Daddy's going! Mind that orange juice!

FRANK *comes in. He is in civvies: a white woollen polo-neck sweater, dark trousers and shoes and a light brown hound's-tooth tweed jacket with a folded newspaper in a pocket.* MIKE *stands as* FRANK *comes towards him and holds out his hand.* FRANK *stops before he reaches* MIKE's *table.*

MIKE. Frank. Thanks for giving Vera a lift. (FRANK *hasnt taken his hand.* MIKE *hesitates.*) The flat seems t' keep her busy. (*No response.*) Policeman must feel funny visitin 'is pal in prison.

FRANK *speaks in a low voice, but naturally so that he doesnt attract attention.*

FRANK. You bastard. That's all.

FRANK *turns and walks away.* MIKE *stares after him. Three-quarters of the way across the room* FRANK *turns and comes back.* MIKE *realises now that* FRANK *is white with anger.*

MOTHER (*off*). Lucile!

FRANK *tries to speak. His anger almost paralyses his mouth. Forces words through his teeth.*

FRANK. You shouldnt be – all you should be – hanged –

pollute the streets. You see me – first word: flat. You didnt
– buy me – duty. Im glad I saw you – your box.

MOTHER (*off*). Look at the state you're in! Your dress!

FRANK. You're not out – your time starts – you're tied to
my eyeballs – Mummy wants Lucy – you look forward –
hands on innocent people – your first move – 's your last.

FRANK *goes.* MIKE *stares after him with a blank face.*

PART THREE

Section One – The Flat – Living Room

*There is no hallway. The front door is downstage right. When
MIKE leaves at the end of the section he unlocks the door from
the inside, goes out and shuts the door, leaving the keys inside in
the lock.*

**Section Two – Ellen's House
'Two Shoes'**

There is no hallway. The front door is downstage right.

Oliver's arrival:
OLIVER *gives his three code rings.* MIKE *and* ELLEN *turn to
stare at the door.* OLIVER *opens it and comes in. He sees* MIKE
and pauses.

Frank's arrival:
FRANK *gives one long ring.* ELLEN *comes from the kitchen
wearing her pinafore.*

ELLEN. You expectin?
OLIVER. Yer bin followed. (*Wolf whistle.*)

   ELLEN *goes to the front door.*

OLIVER. Tell 'em we ain buyin.

ELLEN *opens the door.* FRANK *stands there. She tries to shut
   the door as she turns to* MIKE.

ELLEN. The police –

FRANK *comes in behind her. He wears uniform.*

FRANK (*to* ELLEN). He lodging here?

   (*No other changes in the section.*)

Section Four – Stairway of Ellen's Flats

No stairway. FRANK loiters downstage. His posture shows he is outside. OLIVER has just left ELLEN's flat and is still pulling on his jacket. FRANK stops him.

(No other changes in the section.)

Section Five – Ellen's Living-Room
'Training'

The Grey Room. This is not staged. The whole fight takes place in ELLEN's living-room.

Section Six – Hospital Ward

OLIVER *sits in an adult version of a child's high chair. It has a table top that swings across to hold in the sitter. On it, an invalid's plastic mug with a spout. A drip-feed apparatus is attached to the back of the chair.* OLIVER *wears yellow pyjama trousers and a printed sweat shirt. His head is gauzed unevenly so that parts of it show through.*

ELLEN *sits in the visitors chair.* MIKE *stands at her side.*

(No other changes in this section.)

Section Seven – Ellen's Bedroom

ELLEN *and* MIKE *could undress on stage and lie on a blanket or mattress on the floor.*